跨文化交际实务

Case Study on Cross-Cultural Communication

谢工曲　胡虹　吴瑾　张英◎编著

·广州·

版权所有　翻印必究

图书在版编目（CIP）数据

跨文化交际实务：中文、英文/谢工曲等编著. —广州：中山大学出版社，2022.12

ISBN 978 - 7 - 306 - 07644 - 1

Ⅰ. ①跨… Ⅱ. ①谢… Ⅲ. ①文化交流—汉、英 Ⅳ. ①G115

中国版本图书馆 CIP 数据核字（2022）第 215849 号

出 版 人：	王天琪
策划编辑：	熊锡源
责任编辑：	熊锡源
封面设计：	林绵华
责任校对：	丘彩霞
责任技编：	靳晓虹
出版发行：	中山大学出版社
电　　话：	编辑部 020 - 84110283，84113349，84111997，84110779，84110776
	发行部 020 - 84111998，84111981，84111160
地　　址：	广州市新港西路 135 号
邮　　编：	510275　　传　真：020 - 84036565
网　　址：	http://www.zsup.com.cn　　E-mail：zdcbs@mail.sysu.edu.cn
印 刷 者：	佛山市浩文彩色印刷有限公司
规　　格：	787mm × 1092mm　1/16　11.25 印张　225 千字
版次印次：	2022 年 12 月第 1 版　2022 年 12 月第 1 次印刷
定　　价：	45.00 元

如发现本书因印装质量影响阅读，请与出版社发行部联系调换

序　言

2019年年初,"知乎"上一篇题为《中美医疗水平差距有多大?》的文章指出,中美医疗水平差距在于,中国学生从走进医学院的那一刻起就已经落后了。由于国内的医学基础课教材主要由做科研的教师编写,虽然知识点的讲解全面系统,但是对这些知识与临床实际运用的关系鲜有介绍,学生进入临床阶段前积累的病例极少;而国外的医学教科书主要由临床医师编写,融入大量病例,学完基础课时,学生平均积累2万个病例。这种情况不仅出现在医学教育领域,其他学科也不同程度地存在类似现象。比如,就语言能力而言,许多毕业生手握各种语言考试证书,但在职场上却不懂得如何有效地表达、沟通。

本教材配合"中国企业与中国文化走出去"战略,注重理论与实践相结合,在阐述跨文化交际理论和规律的同时,以多样化的跨文化职场环境中真实的交际场景为核心,重点介绍跨文化交际中遇到的主要问题、成功的解决方案、失败的教训、专业人士的咨询建议等。

本教材精选30多个案例,主要包括国外主流媒体报道的跨国公司海外经营中经历的跨文化冲突、国外跨文化咨询机构的典型案例和专业指导意见、中国企业海外投资调研报告、跨文化交际专业论文等。本教材旨在引领读者走进海外职场,直面跨文化交际中的主要问题,寻求解决方案,力图创造一种身临其境的跨文化体验,积累跨文化工作经验。通过一系列具体案例分析,帮助读者掌握工作语言及其区域文化,深入理解中西方职场文化的差异,缩短接受跨文化冲击的过程,提高学习者的跨文化沟通能力和职场思维能力。

谢工曲

2022年1月5日

目　　录

第一章　文化维度与中西文化差异　/ 1
一、霍夫斯泰德的国家文化维度　/ 1
二、权力距离　/ 1
　Case 1　Status and Respect　/ 4
三、个人主义与集体主义　/ 7
　Case 2　Culture Clash at a Chinese-Owned Plant in Ohio　/ 10
　Case 3　New Documentary Examines a Chinese Factory in the Heart of America　/ 14
　Case 4　Sure, Watch "American Factory", but Don't Think that All Chinese Factories Are like the One in the Film　/ 19
　Case 5　BYD Appoints Two New Managers at Californian Manufacturing Plant　/ 21
　Case 6　Challenges of Localization　/ 23
四、阴柔气质与阳刚气质　/ 30
五、不确定性规避　/ 31
　Case 7　Avoiding Uncertainty in Japan and US　/ 33
六、长期导向与短期导向　/ 35
　Case 8　Significance of Business Relationships　/ 36

第二章　跨文化交际的主要障碍　/ 39
一、跨文化交际　/ 39
　Case 1　International Business—The Cost of Not Being Prepared　/ 39
二、跨文化交际的障碍　/ 43
　Case 2　Asians in US Torn Between Safety and Stigma over Face Masks: Clashing Cultures and Expert Advice Lead to Discomfort and Outright Racism　/ 46
　Case 3　Should I Leave to Go Back to the Culture I Like to Work In?　/ 53
　Case 4　How to Deal with Culture Shock in Your Workplace　/ 54

　　　　Case 5　Culture Shock in a British Workplace　/ 56
　　　　Case 6　Professional Culture Shock　/ 58

第三章　如何提高跨文化交际能力　/ 62
　　一、跨文化交际能力　/ 62
　　　　Case 1　Three Situations Where Cross-Cultural Communication Breaks Down　/ 63
　　　　Case 2　Six Fundamental Patterns of Cultural Differences　/ 67
　　　　Case 3　Nothing Works Better than a Little Competition?　/ 70
　　二、跨文化交际能力的构成　/ 71
　　　　Case 4　Major Corporate Cultural Differences Between Western and Eastern Workplaces　/ 73
　　　　Case 5　East vs. West: Cultural Differences in the Workplace　/ 78
　　　　Case 6　How to Impart Chinese Way of Communication to Dutch Employees　/ 81
　　三、如何培养和提高跨文化交际能力　/ 83
　　　　Case 7　Five Secrets to Meaningful Intercultural Communication　/ 84
　　　　Case 8　Who Is to Pay?　/ 87

第四章　高语境文化与低语境文化　/ 90
　　一、高语境文化与低语境文化的形成　/ 90
　　　　Case 1　High and Low Context Communication　/ 92
　　　　Case 2　Cultural Differences in Business Communication　/ 94
　　二、高语境和低语境折射的中美文化差异　/ 101
　　　　Case 3　Hua Chunying's Answer to Blooberg Reporter (April 11, 2020)　/ 102
　　　　Case 4　Statements on the China-US Trade Meetings　/ 107
　　三、高语境文化在中国企业海外投资中的具体表现　/ 108
　　　　Case 5　Main Obstacles Chinese Companies Face in the Initial Stages of Business Operations　/ 109
　　　　Case 6　Intercultural Communication on Web Sites: A Cross-Cultural Analysis of Web Sites from High-Context Cultures and Low-Context Cultures　/ 113

第五章　时空观念的中西文化差异　／132
一、时间观念　／132
二、空间观念　／133
  Case 1 The Spatio-Temporal Differences of Chinese Enterprises' Experience in the Netherlands　／134
  Case 2 Time Orientation Toward Task or Relationship　／138
  Case 3 Punctuality, Another Way of Acknowledging Rank　／140

第六章　中西商务谈判风格的差异　／141
一、谈判目标的差异　／141
二、谈判策略的差异　／141
  Case 1 International Negotiation: How Do I Get Ready?　／142
  Case 2 Global Contract Practices　／151
  Case 3 Individual Decision Making vs Group Decision Making　／153

第七章　提高信息传播的有效性，讲好中国故事　／157
一、掌握汉英语言表达习惯和文化方面的差异，提高信息传递的有效性　／157
二、将技术写作的原则运用于外宣翻译，加强国际传播的针对性，讲好中国故事　／163

参考文献　／171

第一章　文化维度与中西文化差异

一、霍夫斯泰德的国家文化维度

关于文化，许多学者从不同角度做出了界定与诠释。有人认为，文化包含了人类社会所有的物质产品和精神产品；有人认为，文化主要是指人类社会的制度规则以及社会成员的思想观念；还有人认为，文化主要涉及社会成员的价值观。文化的宏观定义是：文化是人类创造的一切事务的总和，包括物质和精神层面，如语言、哲学、宗教、价值观、社会制度、教育、文学、艺术、建筑、医学、风俗习惯、食品、服饰等。

荷兰心理学家霍夫斯泰德（Geert Hofstede）认为，文化包含两种含义：一种与"文明"同义，是对思想的提炼，包括教育、艺术和文学；另一种含义来自社会学和人类学，指的是社会成员的思维、感情和行为模式等，即社会行为的不成文规则，侧重于社会成员的价值观。处于社会群体中的每一个人都会遵循一套共同的行为模式，而这套行为模式又是分层次的，与人们所处的社会阶层和扮演的角色相适应。同时，不同的行为模式对应文化的不同层次，包括：国家层次、种族层次、宗教层次、性别层次等。

霍夫斯泰德采用社会学的分类法，将不同国家的文化之间的差异归纳为五个基本的文化维度，这五个维度是权力距离、个人主义与集体主义、阴柔气质与阳刚气质、不确定性规避、长期导向与短期导向。霍夫斯泰德的国家文化维度分类反映了不同国家之间的价值观差异带来不同的文化，这一理论便于人们更多地了解不同国家之间的文化差异，增进各个文化之间的相互理解，有助于人们跨越国家之间的文化屏障，更好地为跨文化交流做准备。

虽然这种以国家为单位研究不同文化之间的异同的做法存在不足，因为一个国家境内往往存在差异很大的多种文化，但是，霍夫斯泰德的国家文化维度研究还是具有现实的指导意义的。

二、权力距离

权力距离（power distance）是指人们对社会中权力分配不平等的接受程

度。在高权力距离指数国家，人们普遍能接受权力和地位不平等的存在，并对权力表现出尊重和敬畏，也能接受有些人比其他人更有权力和影响力。同时，人们更期望掌权者能够承担与权力相伴的责任，照顾其下属的利益。掌权者享有最大的话语权和特权，并且尽可能将自己与那些没有权力的人区分开，例如，出席会议、参与活动的座位安排、名片上的称呼、办公室的位置等都是权力地位的象征，而且，与陌生人打交道时的相互问候大都涉及对方的年龄、职业等信息，这其实也是一个确定自己与对方的长幼和尊卑的过程，对不同等级的人，给予不同的面子。工作中，严格按照等级顺序办事，人与人的交往受到各自的地位和角色的制约；家庭中，注重长幼有序，尊卑有别，否则就是失礼。

在低权力距离指数国家，社会等级差别不大，人们认为每个人都享有同等的权力，追求个人目标，实现个人价值，人与人之间平等共处，上下级之间在工作之外也是平等的关系。组织机构中的等级区分主要基于管理的便利，多为扁平化管理，等级越少越好。人们倾向于淡化权力差异，并尽可能地下放和分享权力。

研究数据表明，亚洲国家通常属于高权力距离国家，如新加坡、中国、日本、韩国等国家；而欧美大部分国家则属于低权力距离国家。权力距离在中西文化差异方面表现得十分突出。

在高权力距离国家，这种文化特征在企业的对外传播中也显而易见。例如，在企业形象宣传中常常使用许多体现高权力距离的表述，强调企业的政府背景、权威性、权力和排序等，突出企业在业界的实力和影响力。

（1）…Bank of China served consecutively as the country's central bank…

…the Bank rose to a leading position in the Chinese financial industry and developed a good standing in the international financial community.…

The Bank was listed on the Hong Kong Stock Exchange and the Shanghai Stock Exchange in June and July 2006 respectively, becoming the first Chinese commercial bank to launch an A-Share and H-Share initial public offering and achieve a dual listing in both markets.

（2）China Petrochemical Corporation was established in July 1998 on the basis of the former China Petrochemical Corporation, a move by the central government to strategically restructure the petroleum and petrochemical industry…. A super large petroleum and petrochemical group…it exercises the investor's rights to the related state assets owned by its full subsidiaries… It operates, manages and supervises state assets according to related laws, and shoulders the corresponding responsibility of maintaining and increasing the value of state assets.

而在低权力距离的社会，常常淡化权力距离和等级差异，企业宣传强调服务客户，侧重业务范围和规模，突出企业的愿景——助力个人和客户实现各自的目标和价值，凸显企业担负的社会责任，同时，频繁使用"we""our customer"来拉近企业与客户的情感距离。

(3) Bank of America is one of the world's leading financial institutions, serving individual consumers, small and middle-market businesses and large corporations with a full range of banking, investing, asset management and other financial and risk management products and services. The company provides unmatched convenience in the United States, serving approximately 66 million consumer and small business clients…

(4) We do more than create jobs and pay taxes in the communities where we operate. We listen. Our dedication as a community partner is evidenced in the local events we sponsor. (ConocoPhillips)

(5) At AT&T, we're bringing it all together. We deliver advanced mobile services, next-generation TV, high-speed internet and smart solutions for people and businesses. That's why we're investing to be a global leader in the Telecommunications, Media and Technology industry.

Connect people with their world, everywhere they live, work and play… and do it better than anyone else. So our customers can stay connected from nearly anywhere. It doesn't matter if they're driving home from work or traveling across the country or beyond.

在教育和社会生活方面，在权力距离指数较高的国家，社会成员对不平等的接受程度更高，弱势群体倾向于依赖强势群体。家庭中强调顺从、听话，学校中主张尊重师长，谦虚是一种美德。而在权力距离指数较低的国家，社会成员对不平等的容忍度很低，人们尊崇独立自主的价值观，淡化身份地位，主张平等相待，各抒己见，鼓励个性差异。家庭中，父母与子女关系平等；学校中，师生平等交流，鼓励学生与老师探讨甚至争论，注重培养学生独立、自信、尊重他人的性格及价值观。

在职场，高权力距离指数国家的人们往往更容易接受等级制度，对权力集中、严密监管、较大的收入差距容忍度高，管理者与下属之间的关系近似于家长制，管理者对下属严格要求的同时也带有相当的个人感情色彩，为人情关系留有余地。上下级之间的关系和决策过程更加程序化，上级发布指令，提供答案，下级只需照此执行，不必采取积极主动，并且自动接受严密的监督。在低权力距离指数的国家，人们认为个人在组织中只有分工不同，没有地位高低，组织成员注重权力分散，自主决策，难以容忍组织内过大的收入差距，而且不喜欢受到严密的监督。上下级之间的关系讲求实效，较少带有感情色彩。企业文化中，一定范围内的意见分歧是被鼓励的，下级因积极主动而受到奖励，他们的建议得到重视。

在日本，商务惯例和沟通风格主要依据个人在组织中的地位和头衔进行，员工对上司说话恭敬而正式，不太可能反对或质疑主管的指令。在中国，员工比较遵循等级制度，下级比较顺从上级。但在欧美企业，员工则比较期待平等和共享式的管理方式，尽可能地缩小上下级之间的距离。例如，福耀美国工厂的美国员工抱怨，中国人对员工培训、与美国员工分担责任甚至与美国员工交流互动不感兴趣（the Chinese had little interest in training, sharing responsibility with or even engaging with American employees）。他们也看到了中美企业管理方式的差异：中国工人接受指令，然后马上执行（Workers in China are given orders, and they tackle them）；曹先生的工厂总是从乡村招收员工，他们都比较顺从，而美国工人则期待一种更好的团队管理风格（Mr. Cao often populates their factories with migrants from rural areas, whom they expect to be relatively submissive, unlike American workers, who expect a more collegial management style.）。详见Case 2和Case 3。

Case 1

Status and Respect

[提示]

Case 1涉及的文化差异主要表现在：

1. 在一些低权力距离指数国家，一个人的社会地位和被尊重程度主要取决于他/她的个人成就，例如工作业绩、个人财富或公众认可度，与他/她在某机构中的工作头衔和岗位关系不太大。工作头衔和岗位只是便于界定一个人的工作职责和权力范围。

而在一些高权力距离指数国家，例如，部分拉美国家和亚洲大部分国家，人们更关注头衔、等级和权力，有权力的人通常受到尊重，尽管有些人的个人资质并不高。相反，有些取得重大成就的个人却因缺乏相应的社会背景和头衔而得不到应有的尊重。在这种高权力距离文化中，清晰的等级观念也折射在商业活动和其他领域之中，企业高管受到追捧，并倾向于以家长式的行为方式展示其地位和权威，表现他们的重要性。

2. 与来自不同文化背景的人打交道时，不要想当然地以为自己的行为准则与对方的一样，而是要确保以对方的方式而不是自己的方式赢得对方的尊重和信任，这样双方才能进行有效的商务沟通。例如，在高权力距离指数的文化中进行商务活动，需要借助对方的方式充分展示自己的重要角色和责任范围，让对方相信你的地位与他们相等甚至更高。否则，就不可能进行正式的业务讨论和谈判。这不是肤浅的作秀，而是赢得同行尊重与信任的关键。

Here is a lesson about cultural differences I learned the hard way: I first met Octavio Umberto, a senior manager with a large multinational company, in his native Brazil. We spent hours discussing ongoing business between our companies and getting to know each other. Next, he took me on an extended factory tour, proudly showing me the multitude of goods they produced. He and I got along great. After my trip, we stayed in touch via email on a regular basis.

A year later, I left the Fortune 500 company I had been working for in order to start my own business. Hoping he might be willing to serve as a reference, I contacted Senhor Umberto by email. After there had been no response in more than two weeks, I called him in his office to follow up on my request.

When I stated my name, he immediately hung up.

Senhor Umberto and I had been on good terms up to this point. I was sure that my email to him had been friendly and could not think of anything that might have offended him. Nonetheless, he hung up on me when all I was asking for was a simple favor. What was I to make of this strange and blatantly offensive behavior?

What Constitutes Status?

The answer, I realized, had little to do with Senhor Umberto. Instead, it flags an important cultural difference in what constitutes status and how people respond to it. In the United States, Canada, and to a lesser degree, Western Europe, the recognition a businessperson enjoys largely depends on his or her individual achievements, such as business accomplishments, personal wealth, or public recognition received. Job titles matter only in as much as they help determine a person's responsibility and influence. While a strong educational background is also respected, degrees, even Ph. D. ones, at best receive a passing interest a few years down the road. Respect has little to do with position, since it is commonly assumed that someone who earned respect at one place will also be successful elsewhere, making him or her a person worth staying in touch with. An American not responding to my email might not be signaling anything; he or she might simply be too busy. However, hanging up on my call would clearly signal strong negative feelings towards me.

In Brazil, other aspects strongly influence a person's status and authority, the level of respect the individual receives, and the "rules" for interacting with him and her. This is also the case elsewhere in Latin America, in most of Asia, and in many other countries around the world. Members of these cultures tend to pay close attention to titles, rank, and formal authority. Those in positions of power are usually respected even if their personal qualifications are limited. Conversely, individuals who have achieved significant personal successes but lack the "right" background and title might command little respect. In such strongly authoritarian cultures, clear hierarchies are viewed as essential in business and elsewhere. Executives may enjoy enormous deference and tend to behave in paternalistic ways. They are expected to demonstrate their importance through status symbols and corresponding behaviors.

In my case, Senhor Umberto had accepted me as a business partner because of my previous job title and the formal authority it carried. As soon as I gave up that position, I no longer represented an equal partner within his cultural framework. Since we had not developed a close business relationship either, at least to his standards, he may not only have felt that he had the right to ignore my request for a personal favor, my call might even have offended him. From his perspective, he owed me nothing and saw no reason to do me a favor.

Important to Signal Importance

My experience with Octavio Umberto, whom I still greatly respect, reminded me of an essential lesson: when dealing with someone from a different culture, don't assume that the "ground rules" are the same for both of you. Before making my request, I should have made sure to win my counterpart's respect on his terms, not mine.

Success in status-oriented cultures requires convincing your counterparts that your own status is equal or higher than theirs. Otherwise, serious business discussions and negotiations may be impossible. You may want to put your titles on your business card and other materials, talk about the importance of your role and the extent of your responsibility, refrain from leveling with subordinates, dress meticulously, mention that you are staying at a top hotel, and do whatever else you can to signal status and authority. You may not think much of these "superficialities", but they could be crucial in winning your counterparts' respect. Business cannot be done without it.

(By Lothar Katz. Http: //www. leadershipcrossroads. com/arti_ sar. asp)

Words and Expressions

consecutively	adv.	连续地
reference	n.	推荐人，介绍人
authoritarian	n.	权力主义的
hierarchy	n.	社会等级；社会阶层
deference	n.	顺从，尊重
paternalistic	adj.	家长式作风的
ground rules		基本规则
level with		与……平等
meticulously	adv.	细致地，一丝不苟地
superficiality	n.	表面现象，肤浅的表现

三、个人主义与集体主义

个人主义与集体主义（Collectivism vs. Individualism）是指社会中个人与集体的关系。虽然没有哪一种文化是完全的个人主义或集体主义，但是大多数文化往往偏向于其中一种。每个国家所表现出的个人主义倾向差异很大。个人主义社会强调自主、自信、自由和独立，个人利益高于集体利益。而集体主义社会则强调人与人之间的相互依赖关系，个人行为以社会义务、社会和谐、合作互惠为准则，集体利益高于个人利益。

个人主义社会是一种松散的社会组织结构，人们在心理和情感上彼此独立和疏远，每一个人都非常重视自身的价值与追求，鼓励竞争，人人平等，注重自我表现和个人成就，依靠个人努力实现个人的价值与目标，同时，人们在自愿的基础上互惠互利。虽然个人可以选择加入群体，但其成员身份对个人地位的提升或成功并非必不可少。

相反，集体主义社会是一种联系紧密的社会结构，个人往往被视为群体中的一员，群体成员之间和谐共处，相互依赖程度强，因此需要考虑他人的需求和感受，群体成员之间在心理和情感上相对亲密，但对非群体成员则较为疏远。在集体主义社会中，群体的影响力高于个人，从众心理较强，个人以群体的存在和发展为前提，个人期待群体的关照，同时又积极回报和忠于群体，并以群体为荣，有时，为了群体利益需要牺牲个人利益。个人身份在很大程度上取决于他/她在群体中的身份和角色，尊敬长辈和上级被认为是一种美德，家庭也被视为一个微型社会。

个人权力与群体利益的矛盾贯穿了整个人类社会的发展进程。在个人主义指数高的国家，人们通常以自我为中心，强调个性，突出个人的力量，崇尚个人英雄主义。而集体主义指数高的国家，例如中国，讲究个人与群体之间的协调关系，在以大局为重的前提下，个人利益服从群体利益，崇尚奉献和自我牺牲精神。个人怯于发表不同声音，除非受到群体的鼓励。比起个体的公平公正，集体的安宁和谐更为重要，"沉默是金""吃亏是福""枪打出头鸟""不生事""和为贵"是大部分中国人的思维习惯。

个人主义指数高的国家包括英国、美国、澳大利亚、法国、德国、西班牙等西方国家。相比之下，中国、日本、韩国等东方国家的集体主义精神尤为突出。因此，在2020年新冠肺炎疫情暴发期间，中国人民万众一心，严格禁足和自我隔离，两个月内阻断病毒传播。而在许多欧美国家，"居家隔离"和"公共场合佩戴口罩"只是建议，属于"个人责任"，并非立法，不可强制执行，民众不愿意为了遏制病毒传播而放弃或牺牲各自的生活方式。

研究数据表明，权力距离指数高的国家，个人主义指数往往比较低；反之，权力距离指数低的国家，个人主义指数往往比较高。

在教育与社会生活方面，在个人主义指数较高的国家，家庭教育重视培养孩子的自我意识，孩子成年之后倾向于照顾自己及其核心家庭，亲戚之间的关系比较疏远，公私界限分明。学校教育注重培养学生的自主学习能力和竞争意识，直言不讳受到鼓励。而在集体主义指数高的国家，家庭和学校教育都注重培养孩子的群体意识，群体成员之间相互帮助、资源共享，公私界限比较模糊。人际交往中，注意含蓄谦虚，顾及其他成员的面子，维护群体和谐。一旦出现过失，群体的其他成员都会觉得"丢面子"。

不同文化推崇的价值观也体现在职场上人们的相互关系之中。在个人主义社会，雇主与雇员的关系是基于自身利益的契约关系，维系双方雇用关系的是合同或者契约，谈不上谁对谁忠诚，更不存在谁为谁牺牲，双方都有责任严格遵守并履行合同或契约规定的各项条款，彼此之间谁也不会期待对方有超越合同或契约规定的行为，员工没有义务对企业保持忠诚，为企业奉献与牺牲。企业中，人与人之间的关系较为松散，员工流动率较高。与良好的人际关系相比，个人的现实利益更重要，雇用和晋升的依据是规则和个人能力。商务活动的目的是达成实际的合作内容，通过签订合同实现经济利益。

而在集体主义社会中，雇主与雇员的关系与道德、群体或家庭相关。员工流动率较低，忠诚、奉献与牺牲精神被视为好人品和好员工的重要因素，雇用和晋升看重人际关系，人们重"关系"，要"面子"，维持群体中人际关系的和谐往往比完成任务更重要。"关系"不仅是人与人之间的连接，更是一种相互对等的义务与责任，意味着付出的恩惠可以获取同等或更大的回报。在商务活动中，"关系"是把事情做好的关键，成功的领导者可以巧妙地运用关系快速实现目标。商务交往是为了建立长久的商业伙伴关系，企业通常希望与客户建立长久和谐的人际关系，在商务活动中会安排宴会和多种娱乐活动，增进双方的相互了解和相互信任，以期获得预期的成果。当然，集体主义社会的决策过程通常比较长，相关人员需要交流沟通，解决分歧，一旦达成一致，就会转化为统一的行动力。

因此，在中国企业和机构中司空见惯的加班加点在福耀美国工厂遭到抵制，美国工人坚持8小时工作制（Here, after all, were American workers insisting on limiting themselves to an eight-hour workday），而他们的中国伙伴却要每天工作10~12小时，周末也要加班（The Chinese workers also complain: their American workers are heading home after eight hours while they work 10 and 12 hours and come in weekends）。美国人不能理解为什么中国工人对企业这么忠诚（All the Chinese workers were so loyal to the company. They had this culture of having been trained to dedicate their lives to the company）。又比如，在荷兰的中国企业中，中国外派经理和他们的中国雇员之间的关系可以是亲密的，但也可以是强制性的（The relationship between Chinese expat managers and their local Chinese employees could be intimate yet coercive），虽然这种关系可能会增进管理者和员工之间的相互了解，但如果使用不当，也可能转化为一种权威-下属式或亲子关系式的沟通（While this relationship might enhance the mutual understanding between managers and employees, it could also be exploited, transforming into an authority-subordination or parent-child model of communication）。详见 Case 2、Case 3 和 Case 6。

Case 2

Culture Clash at a Chinese-Owned Plant in Ohio

[提示]

跨文化冲突常常因为价值导向的差异而产生。随着中国企业与中国文化走出去，各种文化冲突和挑战不期而遇，近年来国内外媒体频频报道的福耀集团在美国工厂遭遇的文化冲突就是一个典型例证。中国企业跨国经营遭遇的由文化差异带来的误解与冲突比比皆是，主要表现在语言表达、沟通方式、建立信任的方式、好员工及好经理的标准、经营理念、管理方式、价值观等诸多方面。

Case 2 提及的文化冲突主要表现在：

1. 对于中国投资者来说，企业要生存，效益为先——工会是企业发展的障碍。而对于美国员工来说，他们看重的是工作尊严、安全保障、优渥薪水、不加班、不随意辞退——工会是保障。此外，中国的工会在组织机制和功能运作等诸多方面与美国的工会是完全不同的。

2. 中美企业做事方式不同，对员工的要求不尽相同，对管理者的期待也不相同。例如，"Mr. Cao often populates their factories with migrants from rural areas, whom they expect to be relatively submissive, unlike American workers, who expect a more collegial management style."（曹先生的工厂总是从乡村招收员工，他们都比较顺从，而美国工人则期待一种更好的团队管理风格）。"The Chinese have a bias toward speed; Americans like to process things, think it through from all angles."（中国人更看重速度，而美国人则喜欢从多角度考虑和处理问题。）

MORAINE, Ohio—When a giant Chinese glassmaker arrived here in 2014 and began spending what would become more than a half-billion dollars to fix up an abandoned General Motors plant, it seemed like a tale from opposite land: The Chinese are supposedly stealing American jobs—as no less an authority than President Trump has pointed out.

But now the Chinese were suddenly creating them. More than 1,500 jobs, in fact. The Chinese company, Fuyao Glass Industry Group, decided the money was worth spending in this Dayton suburb to be close to its key customers, the big American-based automakers that buy millions of windshields each year.

And it was not alone.

From 2000 to the first quarter of this year, the Chinese have invested almost \$120 billion in the United States, according to the Rhodium Group (荣鼎咨询), which tracks these flows. Nearly half of that amount has come since early 2016, making China one of this country's largest sources of foreign direct investment during that time.

But with the explosion of investment has come unexpected trouble. At Fuyao, a major culture clash is playing out on the factory floor, with some workers questioning the company's commitment to operating under American supervision and American norms.

Fuyao faces an acrimonious union campaign by the United Automobile Workers and a lawsuit by a former manager who says he was let go in part because he is not Chinese.

The experience of the Fuyao plant shows the potential pitfalls along the way.

The union, which began meeting with workers in 2015, escalated its public efforts in April with a fiery meeting highlighting arbitrarily enforced rules and retaliation against those who speak up.

An employee named Lisa Connolly complained that Fuyao disciplined workers for absences if they didn't request their paid time off far enough in advance, while a former employee named James Martin said the company had exposed him to harsh chemicals that blistered his arms and diminished his lung capacity. (Mr. Martin lost his job for excessive absences while on workers' compensation leave in January.)

Fred Strahorn, the Democratic minority leader of the Ohio House of Representatives, told the audience that Fuyao's operation felt like "a little bit of a hostage situation" and pledged to "show Fuyao that we do things a little bit different in Dayton, Ohio."

In November, the Occupational Safety and Health Administration fined Fuyao more than \$225,000 for violations such as insufficient access to locks that shut down power to a machine when workers fix or maintain it. Such lapses are common in the brutally competitive auto parts industry, said David Michaels, a professor at George Washington University who headed OSHA until January, but they can easily lead to amputation or even death.

The company reached an agreement in March that reduced the amount to \$100,000 and required corrective measures.

Eric Vanetti, the vice president for human resources, conceded an element of turmoil at the plant late last year. But he said that the atmosphere had improved significantly in the past few months and that many of the new safety measures were underway before the OSHA settlement. The company also recently gave hourly production employees a $2-an-hour raise.

Kristi Tanner, a senior official at JobsOhio, the private economic development corporation for Ohio, which helped lure Fuyao to the state, said in a statement that the company "has transformed a long-vacant former G. M. assembly plant and provided an economic lift."

But projects can suffer when investors are unfamiliar with the American regulatory and political environment, as is true for many executives in China, where labor standards tend to be less strictly enforced.

In 2014, a Chinese copper tube maker called Golden Dragon opened a plant in Wilcox County, Ala., to Fuyao-esque fanfare, investing more than $100 million to create an anticipated 300 local jobs. By the end of the year, amid complaints about lax safety and low wages, workers narrowly voted to unionize.

At Fuyao, workers say there have been safety improvements, though some cite continuing problems. One employee, DeAnn Wilson, complained that her area lacks proper ventilation even though she works around machines that emit smoke. (John Crane, Fuyao's health and safety director, said the smoke was vapor that resulted from warm air entering a chilled room.)

Other workers said that despite the company's insistence that it wanted to hand the plant over to American managers, it had increased the proportion of Chinese supervisors in recent months.

That contention is consistent with the legal complaint of David Burrows, who was ousted as a vice president for the plant in November, along with the plant's president, John Gauthier.

"Since those two have been fired, it has more of a Chinese feel than what it was before." said Duane Young, a worker at the plant. He said the Chinese had little interest in training, sharing responsibility with or even engaging with American employees.

In an interview in Beijing, Mr. Cao said he had replaced Mr. Burrows and Mr. Gauthier because "they didn't do their jobs but squandered my money." He lamented that productivity at the plant "is not as high as we have in China", adding that "some of the workers are just idling around."

Athena Hou, the chief legal officer for Fuyao Glass America, called Mr. Burrows's suit "legally meritless". Mr. Gauthier and Mr. Burrows did not respond to requests for comment.

To some extent, cultural norms may explain the tensions.

Mary Gallagher, who directs the Lieberthal-Rogel Center for Chinese Studies at the University of Michigan, said entrepreneurs like Mr. Cao often populate their factories with migrants from rural areas, whom they expect to be relatively submissive, unlike American workers, who expect a more collegial management style. "He hasn't ever had probably this type of pressure from a work force," she said.

Workers at the Fuyao plant say Chinese managers seem to elevate production goals above all else. When employees have trouble with equipment and ask to shut it down, said Nicholas Tannenbaum, a Fuyao worker who was fired in late May, "the Chinese look at us and say, 'No need.'"

"They're jumping on moving conveyors to fix it as the line is running," he added.

Mr. Vanetti, the head of human resources, said the company had not sacrificed safety to meet production targets. But he conceded that "the fundamental difference between Chinese and Americans is that the Chinese have a bias toward speed; Americans like to process things, think it through from all angles."

Mr. Vanetti said that Fuyao remained committed to its original four-to-five-year timetable for handing the plant to a predominantly American management corps, and that it recently hired two more American vice presidents.

(By Noam Scheiber, Keith Bradsher. *The New York Times*. June 10, 2017. Https://nyti. ms/2t5lmz2)

Words & Expressions

expat	*adj.*	（为 expatriate 的简称）外派的
coercive	*adj.*	强制的，高压的
acrimonious	*adj.*	激烈的，尖刻的
pitfall	*n.*	陷阱，圈套
escalate	*vt.*	升级
arbitrarily	*adv.*	武断地，专横地，任意地

retaliation	n.	打击，报复
discipline	vt.	处分，报复
paid time off		带薪休假
blister	vi./vt.	使起疱
hostage	n.	人质
lapse	n.	小错，过失
amputation	n.	截肢
concede	vi./vt.	承认
turmoil	n.	混乱，骚动
regulatory	adj.	管理的，监管的
-esque	suff.	似……的，……式的
fanfare	n.	大张旗鼓的宣传
lax	adj.	不严格的，松懈的
ventilation	n.	通风
contention	n.	观点，争论
oust	v.	罢免，撤职
lament	vi.	哀叹，抱怨
squander	v.	浪费，挥霍
conveyor	n.	传送机，传送带

Case 3

New Documentary Examines a Chinese Factory in the Heart of America

[提示]

Case 3 提及的文化冲突主要表现在：

1. 中美企业对员工的评价标准和要求不尽相同。在中国企业，忠诚、奉献与牺牲精神被视为好员工的重要因素。中国文化注重整体利益，而欧美文化突出个人利益。所以，美国员工无法理解为什么"All the Chinese workers were so loyal to the company. They had this culture of having been trained to dedicate their lives to the company."（所有的中国工人都对企业非常忠诚。他们的文化是为企业奉献自己的一生。）"The American workers complained about being forced to train off the clock."（美国工人抱怨他们在工作时间之外被迫接受培训。）

2. 沟通方式与沟通习惯的差异时常造成误解。例如，中国人在工作中遇到问题时，往往是先解决问题，事后才告知美国同事，而这种沟通方式与美国人先沟通再做事的习惯和风格截然相反。例如，"Workers in China are given orders, and they tackle them. Here in the U.S., workers want to know why they're being asked to do something; they also expect there will be some praise." （中国工人接受指令，然后马上执行。而美国工人想要知道为什么要做某事，他们也期望会得到一些赞扬。）

"American Factory," to air on Netflix, shows three years in the life of Fuyao Glass America erected at the Ohio site of a shuttered GM auto plant.

Americans …

dislike abstraction in their daily lives.

are slow workers and have fat fingers.

live in a culture where children are showered with encouragement, leading to overconfidence.

These are just some of the beliefs about Americans that Chinese supervisors hilariously and alarmingly feed to their Chinese workers. The odd thing is that those briefings aren't taking place in China but in the American heartland: Dayton, Ohio.

So begins American Factory, the intriguing new Tribeca Film Festival documentary (and upcoming Netflix offering) which had its New York premiere on April 26 and was one of five festival films curated by four New York-based film critics.

The story: In 2015, Cao Dewang, chairman of Fuyao Glass America, arrived in Dayton to check out the construction and hiring progress for the U.S. branch of his world-leading automobile-glass company, on the site of a shuttered GM plant. He was attempting to do the seemingly impossible: put Chinese workers to work alongside American workers and meld their two dramatically different cultures.

As filmmakers Steven Bognar and Julia Reichert show, even well-meaning Chairman Cao seemed a tad gob-smacked two years into his bold experiment.

Here, after all, were American workers insisting on limiting themselves to an eight-hour workday; holding an election to consider inviting in the UAW union; and pressuring the company for a rigorously safe factory environment (1,200-degree glass furnaces and the very breakable product they produce being dangerous to human health).

Are the struggles revealed in the film cause for alarm for American entrepreneurs working with or considering partnering with the Chinese companies? "We're not making a promotional film to promote working with China or not working with China," Steven Bognar told Entrepreneur following last week's screening and Q&A.

"We're not trying to make a scary movie," Bognar continued. "We're trying to make a movie about how hard it is. It wasn't easy when the Japanese set up factories here, either, but there are ways you can build bridges or decide not to build bridges."

In 2015, this sudden new influx of jobs, designed to revive that Rust Belt city from its long economic nightmare, are far better than those at the Payless distribution center or at McDonald's. That's why new energy and optimism abound at first in this Ohio city, which once had more automobile manufacturing than any metropolis outside Detroit.

No wonder Chairman Cao wants to document his great project: "The important thing is how this will change the American view of China," Cao says in the film.

"He's kind of a maverick," Reichert said of the chairman during the Q&A. "It wasn't as though many American CEOs would allow filmmakers to be in their plant for three years." GM, she commented dryly, had allowed the filmmakers into its former Dayton plant for a grand total of 20 minutes.

Bognar echoed this upbeat view of Cao, saying "He believes in transparency." That is apropos for a glass manufacturer but it also allowed for amazing insights into the lives of the workers the filmmakers profiled during the factory's first three years. Among them were:

Wong He, a 20-year veteran furnace engineer at Fuyao China who has been brought to Dayton for a difficult two years away from his young family. In Dayton, he lives with four other Chinese men. During the day he's so attuned to working that his "lunch" consists of a packet of Twinkies.

Rob Haerr, a furnace supervisor who invites his Chinese co-workers to his country home for an American Thanksgiving, where the men dine on turkey, try out Haerr's Harley and practice target-shooting using his twin revolvers.

Jill Lamantia, a forklift operator, who was economically felled by the 2008 layoff and recession, but is able, thanks to her new Fuyao job, to move out of her sister's basement. Delight turns to disenchantment, however; and Lamantia becomes a union supporter and is fired for it.

John Crane, a safety manager at Fuyao who grows frustrated at the safety issues at Fuyao and at being forced to lie to Fuyao's automotive company clients. He eventually resigns.

Culture clash among workers

Things quickly went south at the Dayton plant. "All the Chinese workers were so loyal to the company," Lulu Men, a Chinese field producer for the film, said during the Q&A. "They had this culture of having been trained to dedicate their lives to the company. The difference is, Chinese culture is all about unity, and the American culture is about individuality. So I think that made a huge difference, and a culture clash."

Serious injuries proliferated. OSHA fines were levied. American supervisors were replaced by Chinese. The American workers complained about being forced to train off the clock and about their wages—pre-treatment inspector Shawnea Rosser tells the filmmakers she used to make $29-plus an hour at GM; at Fuyao, she says, her wage is $12.84.

The Chinese workers also complain; their American workers are heading home after eight hours while they work 10 and 12 hours and come in weekends. "I think they are hostile to the Chinese," Chairman Cao tells his board members, noting a $40 million loss in the plant's first months of operation.

Another overall difference: "Workers in China are given orders, and they tackle them," Reichert says in the film's production notes. "Here in the U.S., workers want to know why they're being asked to do something; they also expect there will be some praise."

More happily, the film chronicles a big Chinese New Year's party at Fuyao's Chinese headquarters in Fujian Province, to which about a dozen U.S. supervisors are invited. These scenes in the film are somewhat comic to Western eyes: big-bellied Midwestern white men towering over their Chinese bosses. Chinese workers lining up for their morning check-in, in military formation, and singing out motivational company slogans ("To stand still is to fall back.").

Meanwhile, the party itself is an over-the-top three hours of garish costumes, fervent songs about the company's "blessings" and even a wedding of five employee-couples. "We're one big planet. A world somewhat divided but one," a teary-eyed U.S. supervisor says to the camera late in the alcohol-fueled evening.

But back in Dayton, there is no partying. Workers are unhappy. ("Everybody is upset in their own language and everybody just walks away," Lamantia, the forklift operator, says.) The workers set an election to try to bring the union in.

The company, for its part, is not amused, spending $1.25 million to hire the Labor Relations Institute (its motto: "Winning NLRB elections for almost four decades") to dissuade a "yes" vote. Ultimately, the union is rejected, 868-444, but its supporters are fired—an illegal action in the United States, Reichert says, but hardly an uncommon one.

The film ends with flows of workers, Americans and Chinese alike, entering and leaving their shifts. Added in are voiceovers by workers—with comments like, "We're never going to make that kind of [GM] money again," versus, "I believe in the American Dream; we can't give up on that."

Back in China, Chairman Cao is also filmed, making the extraordinary statement that when he looks back on his life's journey from intense poverty and the "Cultural Revolution" to today's capitalism, he asks himself, "Am I a criminal or a contributor?"

"One thing we tried to do is not root this film in Midwestern unease about China," Bognar said at the Q&A. "I think China is a miracle in many ways: Millions of people are no longer in poverty because of this amazing last 30 years. So we hope this movie sparks conversations and gets people talking about these issues, with the hope that they'll focus on people, whether they're Chinese or American."

(By Joan Oleck, Associate Editor. *Entrepreneur*. May 1, 2019. Https://www.entrepreneur.com/article/332981)

Words & Expressions

air	vt.	播出，播放
shuttered	adj.	停业的
hilariously	adv.	引人发笑地；滑稽地
intriguing	a.	引起兴趣的
premiere	n.	首映
curate	vt.	策划
meld	v.	使……合并，使……混合
a tad		有点儿
gob-smacked	adj.	大吃一惊的，目瞪口呆的
influx	n.	大量涌入

maverick	n.	特立独行的人
upbeat	adj.	乐观的，积极向上的
apropos	adj.	恰好的，适当的
attuned to		习惯于
revolver	n.	左轮手枪
forklift	n.	叉式升降机，叉车
disenchantment	n.	希望幻灭
go south		暗指情况越来越糟糕
proliferate	v.	激增
chronicle	v.	翔实记载
tower over		高出，胜过
over-the-top		过多的
garish	adj.	花哨的
dissuade	vt.	劝阻，阻止
shift	n.	轮班

Case 4

Sure, Watch "American Factory", but Don't Think that All Chinese Factories Are like the One in the Film

[提示]
Case 4 报道了中国企业如何与当地工会和社区合作共赢。

Netflix subscribers and theatergoers can now watch "American Factory", a powerful new documentary about what happens when a manufacturing plant opens in a job-deprived town but the plant's owners are callous to workers, hostile to unions and obsessed with profits at any cost.

It is a story that has played out in towns and cities throughout the country for decades. Over a lifetime of advocacy on behalf of workers, I have dealt with numerous company owners who have insisted on their "right" to pay workers poverty wages, bust unions and pollute the environment, just like the owners in "American Factory".

There is a lot the documentary gets right, but there is also something that disturbs me. The film follows the workers at a car glass manufacturing plant in Dayton, Ohio, run by Fuyao, a company owned by a Chinese billionaire. The plant's workers struggle with the outrageous expectations of Fuyao's management (long work hours, lax safety standards, wage cuts), as well as with the culture clash between the differing approaches of workers and managers to production and safety. I won't spoil the film, but don't expect a Hollywood ending.

"American Factory" tells an important and compelling story. But I worry that for some viewers the takeaway will be that this is how Chinese companies operate when they set up shop in the United States. I've seen a lot of manufacturing companies that share many of the worst traits exhibited by Fuyao in the film, and most of them were owned by U.S., Canadian or European companies.

On the other hand, I've also worked closely with a Chinese-owned manufacturing company that couldn't be more different from the one in "American Factory". Like Fuyao, BYD is a Chinese company that opened a plant in the United States—in its case, in the city of Lancaster in northern Los Angeles County's Antelope Valley. BYD builds environmentally friendly buses for city fleets all over the world, including Los Angeles'. The new plant has delivered on its promise of jobs that are beneficial not just for local workers but for all of us living on a rapidly warming planet.

At first, BYD questioned why it was in the company's interest to engage with unions and community groups in the region. But the story of BYD ended differently than Fuyao's does in "American Factory". Workers in Lancaster came together with community members, including union leaders, clergy and environmental advocates, and convinced BYD to do the right thing—for itself and its workforce. Today, BYD is a model employer.

When it comes to the treatment of workers and the protection of the environment, any company anywhere can choose to be a good actor or a bad one—and left unchecked, they often choose the latter. In my experience, nine times out of 10, the key factor determining their choice is whether public officials, workers and local residents have organized effectively to hold the company accountable to fair standards of treatment of workers on the job and protection of the environment. This lesson, rather than anti-Chinese fearmongering, should guide public discussion generated by this important film.

(By Madeline Janis. *Los Angeles Times*. Https://www.latimes.com/opinion/story/2019-08-21/documentary-american-factory-chinese-glass-ohio)

Words & Expressions

subscriber	n.	订阅者，用户
callous	adj.	冷酷无情的
bust	vt.	阻止，破坏，猛烈打击
outrageous	adj.	骇人的，无法容忍的
accountable	adj.	负有责任的
fearmongering	n.	散布恐惧

Case 5

BYD Appoints Two New Managers at Californian Manufacturing Plant

[提示]

Case 5 提及的跨文化沟通主要表现在：

用人本地化，并且全部雇用行业工会会员，加强与行业工会的联系；加强产品质量、生产安全和环境监控，打造企业形象。

The new recruits, Peter Hale and Robert Matute, bring decades of transportation experience to BYD's Lancaster plant in California.

BYD has announced the recent addition of two transportation professionals to its Lancaster, California manufacturing plant team: Peter Hale as Quality Assurance/Quality Control (QA/QC) Manager, and Robert Matute as Safety Manager.

With these two experienced veterans on board, BYD continues its investment in the North American market, critical zero-emission initiatives and ongoing advancement of its plant's production and operational efficiency.

"The appointment of world-class quality control and safety experts like Peter Hale and Robert Matute to our team are additional catalysts in our leadership advancement of this innovative and disruptive market," said Stella Li, President of BYD North America. "We are committed to the highest quality products and experience for our customers as a total solutions provider, and the ongoing, safe workplace for our team."

Hale brings over 35 years of public transit and private sector bus manufacturing experience from the U. S. and overseas, most recently serving for six years as an Assistant Project Manager for the Los Angeles County Metropolitan Transportation Authority (Metro). He served as the technical liaison with OEMs and oversaw new builds of full electric buses, carried out new vehicle inspections for compliance, signed off completed products and served as an overall technical advisor.

As the BYD QA/QC Manager, Hale will oversee BYD's Quality Management System and verify conformance to customer, internal, ISO 9001 and regulatory/legal requirements; inspection of incoming materials; monitoring, measurement, and review of internal processes; and monitoring employee performance, safety and training.

Hale said, "Applying my technical and industry knowledge to BYD's team is one more piece of my journey, and in the evolution of this technology. I am proud to lead a 40-person strong team of quality engineers and inspectors dedicated to keep BYD advancing."

As BYD's Safety Manager, Matute will oversee all aspects of safety, including compliance with local, state, and federal rules and regulations, including California Occupational Safety and Health Administration (Cal/OHSA) and the Environmental Protection Agency (EPA). Helping to maintain a safe workplace, he will develop and implement an updated facility management program including preventative maintenance and life-cycle requirements; provide ongoing safety training and awareness; conduct and document facility inspections; and oversee environmental health and safety.

Matute brings with him more than 20 years of safety management experience in assessing, designing and implementing safety guidelines. Prior to joining BYD, Matute served as the Safety Project Coordinator for the Nevell Group responsible for assisting in the management/administration of the company's corporate safety program. In that role, Matute coordinated the training of workers on safety law and regulations, conducted job site safety inspections, and managed safety documentation.

"My goal is to achieve sustainable, best-in-class, safety performance," Matute said. "We do this by building a strong unified leadership safety culture that engages and empowers employees at all levels to take ownership in reducing unsafe acts and exposure to accidents and injuries. Our actions and behaviors demonstrate that safety is a core value."

BYD is the only electric vehicle manufacturer in the U. S. to have an all-union workforce.

(Https://www.intelligenttransport.com/transport-news/75117/manager-byd-safety-quality-control/ Intelligent Transport)

Words & Expressions

catalyst	n.	催化剂
disruptive	adj.	颠覆性的
public transit		公共交通系统
liaison	n.	联络人
conformance	n.	一致性，顺应
compliance with		符合，遵守
best-in-class		一流的，同类之最

Case 6

Challenges of Localization

[提示]

Case 6 提及的文化冲突主要表现在：

1. 用人本地化和融合两种企业文化的困难。

2. 沟通方式与沟通习惯的差异造成的误解与冲突。中国人的沟通方式比较含蓄，不喜欢直接表达一些负面的信息，特别喜欢用一些微妙的弦外之音来表达，这让西方人难以理解与捕捉。西方人总体喜欢直接，不管是正面还是负面的问题，都喜欢直接表达与面对。

3. 价值观不同。中国企业的人才考核注重考察自我牺牲精神和忠诚度，而西方企业遵循的是劳资双方履行合同和契约规定的各项条款，彼此之间谁也不期待对方有超越合同或契约规定的行为发生。

4. 在中国企业，员工比较遵循等级制，下级比较顺从上级。但在欧美企业，员工比较期待平等和共享式的管理方式。

5. 在中国，工作环境中建立和保持良好的人际关系甚至是亲密关系对完成工作任务至关重要。而在西方，一个人的同事圈和朋友群可以是完全不同的两类群体，工作中，公事公办，对事不对人。

Localization is considered a must by most Chinese companies in the Netherlands. Depending on their specific businesses, the majority of Chinese companies try to employ Dutch local employees and use Dutch banks, legal services, business consultants and accountants. Some of them have also harnessed local marketing and promotion services. In short, using local people and services to develop local business is a formula to success. An SOE manager used a fishing metaphor to explain this. According to him, there were four stages of his company's business development: rod-fishing, net-fishing, fish culture and global operations. Rod-fishing represents an opportunistic attitude, when the fisherman does not know where the fish are located. Using his own words: "If I can sell, I sell. If I cannot sell it here, I switch to another place." Net-fishing is about building a sales network, knowing one's target market and having channels to reach that market. In the third stage, fish culture means further building one's sales channels and creating loyal customers by supporting them with a whole system of after-sales, product development and marketing. The last stage, global operations means "localized research, localized purchase, localized operation and localized financing". These four steps outline a movement from the acceptance of serendipity to control.

This trajectory of development is surely not easy to follow. One interviewee, a Chinese expat manager of a high-tech company, said that he was under a lot of pressure.

Especially when the company needs to develop at such a high speed. On the one hand, the Chinese parent company has a requirement, namely you have to be fast in everything. They are used to high-speed growth. On the other hand, as the manager you need to combine the parent company's requirement with your local situation. We all say, it is not easy to be a manager of our company but it is even more difficult to be the overseas manager of it.

The manager's words highlight two main challenges that most Chinese subsidiaries are facing in the localization process. First, how to attract qualified local employees and integrate different cultures and norms within the subsidiary so that it can run efficiently. Second, how to deal with a demanding parent company.

1. Recruitment

The first challenge on the path to localization is to find the right local employees. This proves to be especially tricky for smaller companies and newcomers. On the one hand, the specific talents they need can be rare in the Netherlands. For instance, a manager stated that his company needs someone who can deal with multiple tasks at the intersection of law, accountancy and finance, since as a small subsidiary in the Netherlands they have to deal with the different departments of their very large parent company. He feels, the Dutch employees are often trained in a specific area but cannot deal with multiple tasks. Another manager whose company specialized in machine manufacturing complained that the most skillful technicians are in Germany. While another manager whose company is in tele-communication sighed that the IT sales and marketing is a newly emerging area and that he could not find suitable Dutch employees in this field.

On the other hand, some Chinese companies observed that the really talented people do not always like to work for a Chinese company. This is not only true for Dutch people but also for Chinese graduates. A Chinese company had its director's position vacant for almost two years before an experienced manager could be found to take the role. Another Chinese manager shook his head and said they rarely have talented people with working experience sending their CVs, although he thinks that the company offers competitive salaries. However, the situation can be very different for specific Chinese companies. Whereas well-established companies such as Huawei have already organized recruitment events and nurture potential talents with their seed-projects, small enterprises are often still relying on Chinese websites such as gogodutch. com to spread the advertisement for enrolment.

Nevertheless, a general trend of hiring more Dutch local employees is discernible. In some cases, with a hundred or so employees, only the three top managers are from China and the rest are almost all local Dutch employees. Local knowledge is considered extremely important in achieving success. Moreover, the Dutch faces symbolically contribute to the company's international profile, as images of white and blonde local employees are extremely popular in Chinese companies' promotion materials.

However, the symbolic function of the employees is more of a plus rather than a necessity in job-seeking. Some of the managers stated that they do not care about the nationality of the employees, as the talent and abilities are the most important issues at hand. Some others, after several failed experiences with ethnically Dutch employees, tend to hire local Chinese employees or try to find Dutch employees who might be able to adapt to the Chinese way of working from those who might not during the interviews. When hiring Chinese local employees, either Chinese graduates from

Dutch universities or Dutch Chinese are preferred. Dutch Chinese have the advantage of speaking both languages, and Chinese graduates know Chinese culture and can be expected to accept a Chinese working style. For Dutch job-seekers, speaking Chinese is an advantage, but what is more important is their expertise, network and work experience.

2. Integration & HR management

Localization brings problems of integration, which manifest themselves acutely in both M&A and greenfield investment cases. Transnational companies are necessarily composed of employees of different nationalities and cultures. Cultural and organizational differences can trigger practical problems, as we have already discussed in the case of different conceptions of time, speed and urgency. Moreover, China's general image as a country producing cheap, low-quality products and political stand contribute to the overall negative impressions of Dutch and European societies towards China.

Integration problems show themselves most conspicuously in the M&A cases. There may very well be considerable solidarity among the original employee's management team, which may even resist the new owner. When Chinese companies purchase a foreign company, they tend to keep the original managing team intact. In fact, the organizational skills and systems are regarded as an important asset of the company. Both of our interviewed cases revealed that Chinese expat managers sent by the Chinese parent companies were not even taking a hands-on leading role of the subsidiaries and were content to let the Dutch management lead the business. The first case that we investigated was originally a North American company. The Chinese expat manager, who took on the role as deputy CEO told us that:

"Our employees might feel proud when they were working for the famous North American company…. Even if they had stopped working for such a company it would still look nice on one's CV …. The famous North American company has a golden aura. It is easier for them to accept an American company than a Chinese one. When it was taken over by a Chinese company, there was a bit of a psychological gap that they had to overcome."

However, according to the Chinese manager, the company is running well and the internal relationship is reported as harmonious, due to the "tolerant and inclusive attitude of the Chinese parent company" in addition to the "professional attitude" of the original managing team. To boost morale, the Chinese manager promoted the parent company within the newly-purchased subsidiary. For instance, achievements and developments at the parent company were widely disseminated. Additionally, competitions among different subsidiaries were organized, in which the Dutch team also participated and won prizes.

In the second case, the integration process appeared to be even more difficult. The company itself had been growing rapidly since the acquisition, according to our interviewee "from a profit of 5 million to 8 million in 2011 and 2012 to more than 20 million in 2014 and nearly 50 million in 2015." However, the original managing team strongly resisted the Chinese management, not allowing the expat manager to be part of the top managing team. Since the purchase, some key managers had to be changed. The CEO was dismissed upon his own threat of resignation. The CFO (chief financial officer) was fired because he did not want to share the full financial report with the parent company. The CTO (chief technology officer) retired and the parent company put a newly employed European employee in charge of international purchasing. After these personnel changes, the conflict calmed down, on the surface at least.

In a half joking, half self-pitying way, the Chinese expat manager who was appointed as the Chief Compliance Officer told us: "We can also look at it from another perspective. If a famous Chinese company would be taken over by a Cambodian company and a Cambodian manager would be sent to manage the Chinese team. Would the Chinese listen to him? Definitely not."

But not all interviewees resigned themselves so easily to the lowly position of China on the hierarchy of nations that this implies. A manager who felt that he was treated as "someone from the Third World" by Dutch colleagues said: "They [Dutch colleagues] should have changed their mindset. If they look at how the situation is now, [we] should be a bit higher than them, in terms of both income and expenditures." By the same token, another manager compared the advanced technology used in China and the comparatively old-fashioned Dutch situation.

"I talked about our AliPay online payment system and they [Dutch colleagues] had never heard of such a thing ... I told them all sorts of things that I can manage using AliPay and my Wechat wallet. I can buy movie tickets, pay my utilities, etc. There is no need for bills, which is just a waste of paper. Our group stopped providing paper documents a long time ago, for some five or six years now. Everything has been digitalised. However, here it is not necessarily so."

In conclusion, Chinese expat managers tend to deal with the challenges of integration within the purchased subsidiaries in three ways, namely great restraint and tolerance; constructive interference; and patience to achieve a change of ethos. The expat managers stressed that the attitude the purchased company has towards the Chinese buyers are not independent from how the Dutch society in general look at China and Chinese investors, but hope that with the further rise of the Chinese economy things may change.

3. Managing international teams

How to manage an international team is another important issue confronting Chinese managers. Most of our interviewed companies are composed of Chinese expat managers, local Chinese employees, Dutch employees, Dutch Chinese employees as well as other internationals. How to build solidarity, balance different needs and expectations, reduce conflicts and misunderstandings are critical for the smooth running of these Chinese multinationals.

In a bad situation, the relationship between Chinese expat managers and their local Chinese employees could be intimate yet coercive, while the bond between Chinese expat managers and their local Dutch employees are often polite but distant. Chinese employees may feel discriminated against. Due to culture affinity, Chinese employees tend to form a more intimate relationship with their managers. While this relationship might enhance the mutual understanding between managers and employees, it could also be exploited, transforming into an authority-subordination or parent-child model of communication. Thus, Chinese employees tend to have a higher work load, work overtime more frequently and are often criticized ruthlessly. In short, Chinese managers tend to assume that Chinese employees succumb more easily to the command-style management methods. However, eager to represent themselves as benevolent managers to the Dutch "outsiders", the Chinese managers often adopt a totally different way to treat their Dutch employees. Therefore, the Chinese employees tend to feel discriminated against in the company.

However, Dutch employees may feel alienated. Many Chinese employers state that it is more difficult to make Dutch employees follow their commands. They tend to ask why and since Chinese managers do not often require a reason to carry out plans designed by their superiors, they cannot always provide a convincing answer for the Dutch employees. Moreover, sometimes things taken for granted by the Chinese employers and employees alike are regarded as weird for a Dutch employee. For instance, a Chinese manager may hope his or her employees embrace the "self-sacrificing attitude", meaning giving up personal interest for the collective wellbeing of the company. Indeed, the managers themselves may be willing to work overtime and to be called by the Chinese parent companies at any time. Although it might be widely understood by Chinese employees, the Dutch employees are not used to this way of thinking and behaving. In fact, supposing that Dutch employees are different, the Chinese managers have often also given up the expectation that they will comply to the Chinese way of doing things.

Language plays a role here too. It is not that Chinese managers cannot express themselves in English, but most of the time their English is not good enough to convey subtle meanings so that their employees would read between the lines. As remarked by one of the interviewees, a Chinese leader rarely gives opinions in a straightforward way. This is the Chinese way of management. The leader will not say "yes, I agree"; or "no, I disagree." He would say, "I am not against it, which means you can try." This way of giving orders might be challenging and frustrating for the lower managers. If they succeed, everyone is happy, but if they fail only they are responsible. While a manager could still use this way of management with Chinese employees, the Dutch would not grasp the subtleties. Therefore, the expat managers must translate the subtleties so that they are clear for their Dutch employees. All this tends to make Chinese expat managers feel it is very difficult to communicate with Dutch employees, which leads to the alienation of Dutch employees within a Chinese company.

(Tianmu Hong, Frank Pieke and Trevor Stam, "Chinese Companies in the Netherlands". *Leiden Asia Centre Press. Report-Chinese-companies-in-the-Netherlands-2017-final-. pdf*)

Words & Expressions

harness	v.	利用，控制
serendipity	n.	意外发现，偶尔事件
trajectory	n.	轨迹，轨道
subsidiary	n.	子公司，附属公司
intersection	n.	交叉
discernible	adj.	看得见的，觉察出的
M&A		合并与收购

conspicuously	adv.	显著地，明显地
solidarity	n.	团结
hands-on		实际的
aura	n.	光环，气场
morale	n.	士气
disseminate	v.	宣传，传播
ethos	n.	（某团体的）精神特质，风貌
coercive	adj.	强制的，胁迫的
affinity	n.	亲和力
succumb	vi.	屈服，屈从
benevolent	adj.	仁慈的
alienated	adj.	被疏远的
comply to		服从，遵从
read between the lines		领悟言外之意
subtlety	n.	微妙之处

四、阴柔气质与阳刚气质

阴柔气质和阳刚气质（Masculinity vs. Femininity）的划分，源自对社会性别角色的区分。阴柔/阳刚气质或指数高的社会又被称之为女性化社会/男性化社会。女性化社会关注和谐的人际关系和生活质量，重视与他人合作，在享有自由的基础上，更多地强调公正公平等，对不确定性更加包容，例如北欧国家和多数拉丁语系国家。而男性化社会注重的是成就感、英雄主义、冒险精神和扩张主义。阳刚气质指数较高的国家包括日本、英国、法国、美国、德国、中国等国家。

男性化社会以更加传统和保守的方式定义性别角色。男人要坚强自信，追求工作业绩，实现个人抱负；女人要温柔善良，照顾家庭。男女分工明确，往往"男主外，女主内"。在教育方面，男性化社会对男女学生的要求也不同，甚至学习科目也有区别，人们重视学习成绩，强调竞争和表现自我。

相反，女性化社会更注重情感，人们富于同情心，强调社会福利、生活质量、和谐关系，认为工作是为了更好的生活。两性的社会性别角色互相重叠，界限不明显。家庭中，男女没有明确的分工，双方共同承担家务，对男孩和女孩的要求也没有明显的区别。在教育方面，女性化社会对男女学生一视同仁，尊重学生的学习兴趣和需求。

在职场，男性化社会崇拜强者，强调竞争、刚劲、权力、成就和社会地位，注重表现自我，认为工作是男性不可或缺的事业，生活的目的就是为了成就事业。而对于女性，工作则可有可无，或是承担辅助性的角色，女性较少有机会担任高级管理职位。男性一般不会从事固有观念中多为女性从事的工作，反之亦然。遇到冲突时较少做出让步，态度坚决，咄咄逼人。

而女性化社会重视男女平等，工作类型没有明显的男女区别。在组织结构中，女性担任高层职位的比例相对较大，决策更加强调共识和妥协。遇到冲突时，往往会做出适当调整或让步，注重营造和谐氛围，女性的这些特质有助于使其成为成功的谈判者。而男性特质在谈判中所表现的坚决果断，可能将对方推向更加敌对的立场。

中国文化和英美文化都具有较强的男性化倾向，追求财富和事业成功，甚至可以因为事业忽略家庭和个人生活质量。中国企业通常以企业排名和赶超世界先进水平的雄心彰显企业的核心竞争力和进取精神。

研究表明，欧美企业更擅长运用女性化社会的价值观，例如：强调企业的社会责任，男女平等，强调提高生活品质等价值观（所谓 non-commercial value，非商业价值），强调塑造良好的企业形象。注意下面一些对企业的描述。

(1) Across our 30 countries of operations, over 17,000 men and women work in a truly integrated way to find and produce oil and natural gas. (ConocoPhillips)

(2) The National Association for Female Executive recognized Bank of America as one of their 2015 Top Companies for Executive Women....

(3) Aetna hires its first home office female employee, Julia, a telephone switchboard operator....

(4) Employees received necessary training and development to help them reach their career goals....

(5) Our innovative, collaborative efforts yield products that improve quality of life globally....

(6) Our dedication as a community partner is evidenced in the local events we sponsor.

五、不确定性规避

不确定性规避（Uncertainty Avoidance）是指一个社会对不确定性和模糊情境的畏惧程度，并且通过一系列措施和制度等途径来消除这些不确定性及模糊情境可能带来的风险和不良后果的倾向。通常，东方国家对避免不确定性的需求相对较高；而西方国家长期受到历史传统中的探索和探险精神的影响，特别是欧洲部分国家，对避免不确定性的需求相对较低。

不确定性规避指数高的社会对现实中可能出现的不确定性非常敏感和焦虑，并尽可能通过制定更多的法律、规则、政策和程序加以限制和控制。在这样的社会，人们做事讲究程序，审慎稳重，惧怕风险，习惯按照规矩和计划做事，更相信权威，愿意通过权威的意见和专业知识规避不确定性，同时，人们也有很强的从众倾向，努力减少未知因素或非常情境出现的频率。相反，不确定性规避指数低的社会，适应变化，喜欢冒险，讨厌过多规则，对于不寻常的突发事件较能接受。这类国家包括美国和一些北欧国家。

研究表明，在不确定性规避指数较高的社会和国家，人们具有更高程度的紧迫感和进取心。例如，中国社会的不确定性规避指数较高，主要表现在人们注重家庭储蓄以应对养老看病和其他突发事件，注重对子女的教育投入，旨在帮助他们在人生起跑线上更好地起跑并提高他们的竞争力，在择业上，更倾向于选择低风险的行政机关、事业单位和国企。

日本也属于不确定性规避程度较高的国家。一个典型的实例是，日本在制造业实施"全面质量管理"（TQM）大获成功，因为，"全面质量管理"是一种结构严谨的全方位组织管理方式，是一个不断发现、减少或消除错误的持续过程，旨在使所有参与生产过程的人对最终产品或服务的整体质量负责（TQM is a structured approach to overall organizational management. TQM is an ongoing process of detecting and reducing or eliminating errors. TQM aims to hold all parties involved in the production process accountable for the overall quality of the final product or service.）。

在教育和社会生活方面，在不确定性规避指数较高的社会，人们倾向于认为生活中的不确定性和差异性是一种风险，令人焦虑不安，故要采取一切措施尽可能消除它，在家庭生活中表现为对禁忌、规定和生活细节一丝不苟。在学校教育中注重系统化学习，老师被视为相关领域的专家，负责为学生答疑解惑，提供正确答案。

而在不确定性规避指数较低的社会和国家，例如，在多数西方国家，人们更倾向于随遇而安的生活，鼓励冒险，对不寻常的突发事件较能接受，对不同观点较能容忍，没有刻板的行为准则。在家庭中，对禁忌和规定并不严格，家庭氛围比较宽松随意。在学校教育中，学习方式比较灵活开放，老师不一定要提供最终答案。

在不确定性规避指数高的社会，在职场中，管理层崇尚严密的组织体系，关注日常运营，决策过程中重视专家意见，尽可能消除不确定性。在不确定性规避指数低的社会，管理层更关注组织的发展战略。由于管理者对不确定性并不排斥，所以控制机制并不严密，推行目标管理，个人的主动性能够在组织中得到有效发挥，企业家更容易得到组织成员和管理者的支持。

Case 7

Avoiding Uncertainty in Japan and US

Uncertainty Avoidance

The field of intercultural study owes much to Dutch professor Geert Hofstede's research. One of his important contributions with practical business relevance is that he defined a cultural characteristic he called Uncertainty Avoidance (UA), described as "the extent to which the members of a culture feel threatened by uncertain or unknown situations". It can have interesting implications on the quality and reliability of products made in a country.

No Chance for Chances in Japan

Anyone who has ever traveled to Japan will immediately recognize the concept of Uncertainty Avoidance. This country's culture has very little tolerance for any kind of ambiguity. Leaving Tokyo Airport, one can see large displays showing the current temperature with half-degree accuracy. Buses and trains are expected to follow their schedules to the minute, and even small delays will become the subject of concerns and discussions. Business meetings follow elaborate procedures, often take a long time as seemingly little details are scrutinized, and end with all parties signing detailed protocols to leave no room for misunderstandings. Similarly, when presenting a proposal one needs to give the Japanese side ample opportunity for investigation, risk assessment, and clarification before discussing next steps. These examples reflect a strong cultural characteristic: for the Japanese to be effective, they first strive to eliminate all uncertainties.

This extreme UA preference has helped Japan in achieving its leading role in all aspects related to product quality. Made in Japan, once a synonym for cheap and poorly made products, today is a recognized symbol for excellent product quality and reliability. It can be eye opening to experience how the Japanese UA mentality shapes their quality philosophy. Its influence can be seen in almost all their business practices and reaches far beyond methodologies. At the heart of it is the Japanese belief that a risk they do not understand, and thus cannot manage, is a risk they cannot tolerate.

Project managers in more uncertainty-tolerant cultures like the United States often employ a triage-like risk management concept, categorizing risks as either unacceptable, manageable, or as irrelevant. The latter is often a judgment call: if a risk has a low probability of occurring while common wisdom or past experience say that it will likely not cause a problem, project leaders may choose (sometimes without any further analysis) to assume that the risk can safely be ignored.

This concept is foreign to the Japanese who will not tolerate any "assumed non-risks". All risk factors, no matter how large or small, will have to be identified, assessed, and managed throughout a product's lifetime in Japan. This approach naturally enforces a much more systematic risk assessment and tracking process, promoting superior product quality and reliability.

Implications

The Japanese share their strong attention to details with other high-UA cultures such as South Korea, France, and Germany, albeit to a lesser degree. In product development, critics often label the resulting behaviors as perfectionism, implying that it leads to "over-designed" products and long time-to-market. One but needs to point to Japanese product development cycle times, frequently among the best in the world, to debunk this myth.

Note that uncertainty avoidance does not equal risk avoidance. The Japanese and others are very willing to take calculated risks as long as they understand them well. They will often develop a "Plan B" as part of their risk management.

Lastly, it is important to note that a high UA preference does not necessarily stimulate a strong focus on product quality. For instance, many Latin American cultures have a low tolerance for ambiguity. In their cases, UA mostly shows in the role hierarchies and formalities play in the countries' societies rather than in product development and manufacturing.

So, are there any among the world's emerging economies whose UA culture might also promote high product quality? One stands out: China. Up until recently, it lacked the technology required to achieve high standards. That is changing fast.

(By Lothar Katz. 2005. *Leadership Crossroads TM. Http://www.leadershipcrossroads.com/arti_oua.asp*)

Words & Expressions

elaborate	*adj.*	复杂的，详细的
scrutinize	*vt.*	详细检查
protocol	*n.*	协议，议定书
synonym	*n.*	同义词
triage	*n.*	检伤分类，伤员验伤分类
time-to-market		上市时间
debunk	*vt.*	揭穿真相
calculated risks		预期风险

六．长期导向与短期导向

长期导向与短期导向（Long-term Orientation vs. Short-term Orientation）体现了一个民族是注重长远利益还是近期利益的价值观。长期导向注重长远利益，为了实现终极目标而持之以恒，坚忍不拔。短期导向看重眼前利益和近期效果。长期导向国家包括中国、日本和许多东南亚国家，人们愿意为实现最终目标而不懈努力和奉献。特别是日本，坚持了30多年持续一贯的发展战略，从廉价消费品生产国华丽转身为高品质产品和服务的主要供应商。短期导向国家包括非洲、英国、加拿大、美国等国家，人们更注重当前的生活和享受，不愿为了将来而牺牲眼前利益。

中国属于长期导向国家，中国文化强调奉献、耐心、坚持和眼光长远，反对"鼠目寸光"，急于求成，要"放长线钓大鱼"，注重长期稳定发展。而在西方文化中，耐心几乎等同于缓慢，目光长远就有可能忽视近期的机遇，西方人有时很难看到耐心和坚持的价值，他们更喜欢立刻和快速，而不是谨慎和持久。例如，西方的商业计划通常是每年进行一次，任何超过3~5年的时间框架都被视为长期；与此相反，中国人通常会在更长的时间框架内做计划，谋远虑，有时甚至跨越几代人。这种眼光长远与坚持和耐心也体现在中国文化的方方面面。

在职场，长期导向国家，例如中国，管理者通常喜欢培养人才，注重建立和维护人际关系，愿意进行长期投入以达到最终获益的目的。而在短期导向国家，例如许多西方国家，管理者擅长选拔人才，对所有商业伙伴一视同仁，不会特别注重培养人际关系。

长期导向与短期导向在维护合作伙伴关系方面的差异可见一斑。

Case 8

Significance of Business Relationships

Humans universally prefer to deal with people they know and trust. It seems intuitively obvious that the strength of the relationship between parties conducting business influences their willingness to compromise, collaborate, and seek win-win solutions, all of which makes the cooperation more productive. Business interactions are generally more predictable, effective, and dependable with trusted partners than with strangers. Nevertheless, members of different cultures seem to be drawing vastly different conclusions from these findings. Analyzing the overall role relationships play in their business practices, we can identify four different groups of cultures.

Business relationships are moderately important.

Members of cultures belonging to this group, which includes Americans, Australians, Austrians, Canadians, Germans, and others, rarely view strong relationships a necessary precondition for business interactions. Being task-oriented, they tend to focus on business objectives. Their primary motivators are often near-term financial or strategic benefits rather than long-term relationship aspects. Though they may expect to get to know the other party better while doing business together, they do not need to trust someone in order to make a deal with him or her. Many in this group are reluctant to invest significant time and effort into relationship building during the early stages of business engagements. In addition, business ties exist mostly at the corporate level: if a new company representative is introduced into an existing relationship, that person is usually soon accepted as a valid business partner.

Business relationships are important.

These cultures tend to value trust between business partners more highly than those in the previous category do. While they may also engage in deal making without first getting to know their counterparts, members of this group will strive to learn much more about them over the course of the exchange. Once initial interactions have been successful and trust has been established, a sense of loyalty may develop, facilitating future business engagements. Relationships still mostly exist at the corporate level with this group, but individual employees usually also aim to strengthen personal ties with their business counterparts. These characteristics apply to many European cultures, among them Finland, France, Hungary, Northern Italy, Poland, Switzerland, the United Kingdom, and others.

Business relationships are very important.

People in this group of cultures, which includes Indians, Hong Kong Chinese, Koreans, Mexicans, Pakistanis, Russians, Saudi Arabs, Southern Italians, and Spaniards, as well as most Latin Americans, value lasting and trusting business relationships. They prefer to do business with those they know and like. Accordingly, they are prepared to spend significant time building and strengthening relationships. Usually not interested in near-term deals, they mostly focus on longer-term engagements and repeat business. Because potential business partners may first have to prove themselves trustworthy, initial engagements could be small, especially with foreigners. When members of this group engage in business interactions without first spending time to get to know their counterparts, this likely indicates that they are seeking quick gains and are not interested in longer-term business with the other party. The concept of corporate relationships does not mean much to this group. Since business is viewed as personal, individuals expect to spend considerable time and effort to develop close ties with their immediate counterparts even when their companies have a long history of doing business together.

Business relationships are critically important.

Members of cultures belonging to this group, among them Asian countries such as China, Indonesia, Japan, Malaysia, the Philippines, as well as countries such as Brazil, Egypt, or Greece, prefer to build deep and lasting relationships with prospective partners before entering into serious business engagements. They may expect to continue developing such relationships into true friendships as the business partnership continues. Both sympathy and trust are essential requirements for them to make deals with others. With this group, it is vital to be prepared to spend considerable time and effort building strong relationships throughout the business exchange. With the exception of the Japanese, who seem equally focused on tasks and relationships, members of this group may appear less task-oriented than others may. They do not pay much attention to contracts, since most of them believe that the strength of business relationships matters much more than "a piece of paper" does. Keeping in touch with them on a regular basis will ensure that commitments be kept and opens doors for additional business. Since they mostly focus on long-term engagements and repeat business, decision makers may agree with initial deals that appear unfavorable for them, expecting their new partners to make up for this down the road. People in this group pay little attention to corporate-level connections, since few of them believe that business relationships can be successful without strong personal ties. While the more pragmatic members of them may also engage in business interactions with relative strangers if the prospects are sufficiently attractive, they will most likely focus on short term benefits and might not shy away from taking unfair advantage of the other party if given a chance.

These characterizations provide several clues as to what to expect and where to focus your energy when conducting business with people from foreign countries. However, be careful not to take these characterizations at face value. They apply only to business areas that are not critically dependent on personal relationships. In some industries, such as banking, financial services, or legal counseling, the nature of business interactions requires strong trust between the parties involved irrespective of their cultural background. Such a requirement may promote different practices in these industries. In any case, spending time and effort to build closer relationships in international interactions is always conducive to business and therefore strongly recommended regardless of cultural background and type of business.

(By Lothar Katz. Http://www.leadershipcrossroads.com/artibrs.asp)

Words & Expressions

intuitively	adv.	凭直觉地
facilitate	v.	使更容易，促进
commitment	n.	承诺，投入
down the road		未来，一段时间之后
pragmatic	adj.	务实的，实用主义的
shy away from		回避，羞于
irrespective	adj.	不顾的，不考虑的
conductive to		有益于……

第二章 跨文化交际的主要障碍

一、跨文化交际

跨文化交际（Intercultural Communication）是指具有不同文化背景的个人和群体之间的交际，是人与人之间的信息流动与分享。当今，商业和通信领域正在跨越社会、政治、地理和文化的边界，将世界各地的人们、思想和生活方式联系在一起。这一过程涉及理解、不同的观念、心态、信仰、专业规范、生活方式，以及沟通策略。从语言、手势、言谈举止、风俗习惯到权力体系，各种文化之间都可能存在差异，通过有效的跨文化交流来解决这些差异是一种技能。

跨文化交际一般分为两种类型：语言交际和非语言交际。语言交际主要由口语和书面语构成，通过词语组合传递信息。非语言交际通过行为举止和交际环境传递信息，例如，空间、时间、姿态、手势、动作、眼神、表情、物品、服饰等。非语言交际有助于清晰地传递信息，甚至传递不同的信息。

跨文化交际能力不足会给来自其他文化的人带来伤害，特别是对于从事跨国经营、跨领域服务的人更是如此。人们总是基于自己的文化解读他人的文化，因此，你传递信息的意图与对方接受的信息可能完全不同。文化差异可能造成信任危机和巨大的商业损失。

Case 1

International Business —The Cost of Not Being Prepared

[提示]

Kirk Kerkorian 为什么会起诉 Daimler Chrysler？Microsoft 在南美和阿拉伯世界拓展业务，遭遇的文化冲突主要表现在哪些方面？

What's the cost of not being familiar with a foreign culture your company is engaging in?

How about a billion dollars? After all, that's how much American mega-investor Kirk Kerkorian sued DaimlerChrysler for after their German chairman, Jürgen Schrempp, had bragged in a *Financial Times* interview that the merger between the two companies, officially promoted as a "merger of equals", was really no more than a takeover. The case is still in court, but a similar class-action suit by other investors has already been settled by the company for $300 million. Technically, the issue was a legal one. Practically, however, what got DaimlerChrysler into trouble was that Schrempp lacked the cultural sensitivity and experience to realize that in the US, one simply won't get away with that kind of two-faced behavior. The same act would expectably have much less dramatic consequences in his home country. In fact, it didn't have any.

Microsoft reported losing several millions of dollars in India, the Arab world, and in South America because of cultural mistakes in some versions of their Windows program. Incorrect maps, poor translations that introduced offensive language, and other inappropriate material offended locals and in some cases led to government action. The company had to recall the affected versions, replacing huge quantities of its software packages. A spokesman admitted that "some of our employees, however bright they may be, have only a hazy idea about the rest of the world". As a consequence, Microsoft now sends their staff to dedicated training classes.

Fortunately, most cross-cultural blunders are less severe, or at least less costly, than in these examples. Nevertheless, the list still goes on and on about how businesses waste money and miss opportunities because of a lack of international experience or preparation.

What Goes Wrong

There are three fundamental ways in which international business interactions and engagements fail or become more costly than they ought to be:

1) Failure to cross the culture gap. The interaction falls apart because the parties involved are unable to bridge the culture gap between them. Many negotiations end at this stage. "They asked way too much", "they expected us to accept the short end of the stick", or "you just couldn't trust these guys—they never lived up to their promises" are statements one might hear at the end of such failed attempts. Most of the time, these can be traced back to poor mutual understanding and faulty initial assumptions rather than bad intentions on either side.

2) "Coopetition". The cross-cultural interaction limps along, but the parties

involved fail to communicate effectively and to build sufficient trust between them. As a result, the competitive element outweighs the cooperative one, introducing issues over contracts terms, intellectual property, budgets and payments, and so on. This case is both more common and more devastating than the previous one. Rather than adding value to a company's global business strategy, such an engagement can become a major distraction from its key objectives and cause a lot of damage.

3) Limited collaboration. The parties involved establish reasonable ways to communicate and interact. However, they never fully trust each other. In many foreign cultures, people will not make any major business commitments unless a strong business relationship has been established and they feel that the partner can be fully trusted. Americans may be more at ease here because its culture encourages a competitiveness that maintains an element of rivalry business partners are used to. Dealing with foreign partners thus represents a bigger challenge if the goal is to achieve extensive collaboration.

Common Causes

Six elements can be identified that make or break the success of a global business interaction. All of them are ultimately linked back to people's cross-cultural understanding (or lack thereof).

1) Strategic Objectives

Many international business interactions suffer from poorly defined objectives. Strategy, goals and approach all need to be set with the target culture(s) in mind. Only if strategic objectives and tactics are well aligned with the other culture's values, strengths, and preferences can a long-term gain be realized.

2) Approach

Like any other aspect of running a business, success in cross-cultural interactions requires properly planning the approach. Strategic objectives need to be translated into a plan of action that defines steps, timing, roles, and responsibilities. That plan must also take into account the specific preferences and sensitivities of the targeted culture. Ad-hoc approaches in foreign countries have a very limited chance of success.

3) Negotiation

Negotiating in a different cultural context is one of the toughest challenges in international business. What is effective and what is considered inappropriate varies greatly between countries. At the same time, the stakes are usually high and mistakes costly. Sending one's best and most skilled negotiators won't help much unless they are well-prepared. If they lack a thorough understanding of the other culture, the company may be in for a business disaster.

4) Leadership

Once a cross-cultural engagement is under way, visionary leadership becomes pivotal. Leaders will need to consistently demonstrate that they are serious about the engagement and willing to work through the cultural differences. That takes a strong commitment as well as the skills needed to identify sensitive areas and to act appropriately to build and maintain trust. Executives or middle managers who maintain an "us-versus-them" attitude can cause huge damage. Extensive communication, both within the own camp and with the foreign side, is also essential and requires constant leadership attention.

5) Facilitation

The importance of relationship and trust building triggers a need for proper facilitation throughout the engagement. While early in the interactions senior leaders often drive the progress, they may have to become less involved once the engagement is under way. At that point, it becomes essential that a facilitator be assigned who continues to build the relationship. Sending an expatriate who lives in the foreign country can be very effective, but only if he or she is sensitive and well familiar with the specific culture. Companies not paying attention to this aspect frequently find their employees inadvertently triggering confrontations that hurt the business relationship.

6) Team Preparation

Well-defined strategy and good leadership are not enough to make global business interactions successful. Getting buy-in from all team members involved is also essential. Without proper preparation for the engagement, cooperation will likely be poor and concerns may prevail. The objective has to be to get both sides into the right mindset, opening up to the engagement as an opportunity rather than viewing it a threat. Again, it will be very important to understand and address any cultural differences. Aspects such as how to motivate a team can differ significantly and may dictate a new approach in a foreign culture.

Conclusion

As Globalization accelerates business around the world, companies are realizing that proper preparation for international business is a mandatory step that has a strong positive impact on the bottom line. Effective communication and trust building are the primary factors in making a foreign engagement successful. They are influenced by several elements that take careful planning and orchestration. While this requires significant efforts, it is critical to the business success, and the tradeoff between costs and benefits is clearly favorable.

(By Lothar Katz. Http://www.leadershipcrossroads.com/arti_nbp.asp)

Words and Expressions

class-action		集体诉讼
dedicated	adj.	专门的，专用的
blunder	n.	错误
the short end of the stick		不公平的待遇；不利的处境
live up to one's promise		遵守诺言
limp along		进展缓慢，艰难进行
ad-hoc		临时的，专门的
stake	n.	风险
be in for		必定遭到
pivotal	adj.	关键的
inadvertently	adv.	无意地，不经意地
buy-in	n.	补仓、双赢、认同
mandatory	adj.	强制性的
orchestration	n.	协调地结合起来，编排
tradeoff	n.	权衡，折衷方案

二、跨文化交际的障碍

跨文化交际中，一些隐形的障碍（Potential Problems）会阻碍人们获得跨文化交际的能力，看清这些问题可以避免跨文化交际的失败。

（一）民族优越感

民族优越感（Ethnocentrism）是关于自己的文化群体优于其他文化群体的信念，即把自己的国家看作世界的中心，习惯性地用自己民族文化的标准和实践来评判其他民族或群体。民族优越感具有一定的普遍性，因为所有人都倾向于把自己的群体和文化视为样板，作为评判其他文化群体的标准，自觉或不自觉地从自己文化的角度来分析研究其他文化。因此，民族优越感是跨文化交际中最常见的问题。而实际上，各种文化之间并没有对错与优劣之分。

（二）刻板印象/文化定式

刻板印象，或文化定式（Stereotypes）是人们基于先前形成的观点和态度对某些群体或个人持有的信念或看法，也就是人们广泛接受的观点，是一种对日常生活中接受的信息进行分类和处理的方式。

刻板印象是一种复杂的信息分类形式，它帮助人们提炼与组合以往经验，对特定群体的行为进行预测并做出相应反应。刻板印象妨碍跨文化交流，因为刻板印象倾向于将某些个人的行为或图像组织成简单而固定的类别，并将其假设为一个群体中所有成员都具有的共同特征，从而模糊或忽视人的个体特征。刻板印象还会导致对事物的泛化、简单化或概念化的看法，从而忽略具体环境下的个体特征。此外，人们一旦形成了某种刻板印象就很难将之抛弃，因为人们很容易记住那些符合刻板印象的信息，忽视与刻板印象对立的信息。

这种固定模式的思维方式会导致问题频出。负面的刻板印象甚至会导致对其他文化群体的偏见、怀疑、不宽容或仇恨。刻板印象的形成与传播方式有很多，特别是媒体擅长以固有形式描述某个文化群体。

例如，西方人对亚洲人戴口罩的刻板印象和偏见在2020年初新冠肺炎疫情防控期间达到极致。传统上，西方社会认为只有被感染的人才应该戴口罩，但健康人不需要。如今，这种固执已经让西方社会付出了惨重代价。

"Traditionally, Western societies believe only those infected should wear face masks because they could spread the virus, but healthy people do not need to do so."

"In the U.S., wearing a face mask when healthy has become discouraged to the point of becoming socially unacceptable. The U.S. government, in line with World Health Organization recommendations, says only those who are sick, or their caregivers, should wear masks."

然而，在亚洲，人们在许多情况下都需要佩戴口罩，例如：

Even before the coronavirus outbreak, masks were a common sight across East Asia—worn for a variety of reasons. It's common for people who are ill and want to protect the people around them to wear masks. Others wear masks during cold and flu season to protect themselves.

In Japan, people wear masks for non-medical reasons ranging from wanting to hide a swollen lip or a red nose during allergy season, to keeping warm during the winter, says Mitsutoshi Horii, a sociology professor at Japan's Shumei University, who works in the United Kingdom. Masks in Japan come in cloth and printed variations, and can also be worn for style. They can also be seen on the streets of Hong Kong.

The difference in perception of the mask comes down, in part, to cultural norms about covering your face, he says. "In social interactions in the West, you need to show your identity and make eye contact. Facial expression is very important."

(Hillary Leung, "Why Wearing a Face Mask Is Encouraged in Asia, but Shunned in the U.S." Https：//time.com/5799964/coronavirus-face-mask-asia-us/)

（三） 偏见

偏见（Prejudice）是对一个群体中所有或大多数成员的不公平、有偏见或贬损的态度。它包括种族主义、性别歧视、年龄歧视等。有些偏见显而易见，但有些却难以察觉。偏见使人不能正确地看待或面对现实，常常导致对他人的不公和歧视，在极端状况下甚至可能导致公开的身体攻击。与刻板印象一样，偏见一旦形成就很难被消除。

民族优越感、刻板印象和偏见都会直接影响跨文化交流。例如，2020年新冠肺炎疫情暴发时期，拥有世界一流科研机构和医疗系统的欧美国家成为全球病毒风暴的中心。究其原因，一个重要因素就是，西方国家一直对中国体制和医疗系统充满偏见，甚至对于阻断病毒传播行之有效的封城措施（lockdown）都会采取双重评价标准，例如，*New York Times* 将武汉封城描述成"给人民生活和个人自由造成巨大损失"，而米兰和威尼斯封城却是"承受着经济风险，竭力遏制欧洲最严重的新冠病毒暴发"：

"To fight the coronavirus, China placed nearly 60 million people under lockdown and instituted strict quarantine and travel restrictions for hundreds of millions of others. Its campaign has come at great cost to people's livelihoods and personal liberties."

"Breaking News：Italy is locking down Milan, Venice and much of its north, risking its economy in an effort of contain Europe's worst coronavirus outbreak."

面对来自中国的疫情信息和世界卫生组织发出的警告，素以理性思维、实证为据的西方世界全然无视，痴迷于对民主自由制度的绝对自信，想当然地认为中国的疫情无非是由落后的医疗水平导致的，新冠病毒对于欧美民众来说只是一个大号流感，从而错过了控制病毒传播的最佳时机，直至死亡惨重，欧美国家才恍然大悟。

Case 2

Asians in US Torn Between Safety and Stigma over Face Masks: Clashing Cultures and Expert Advice Lead to Discomfort and Outright Racism

[提示]

亚裔美国人对是否应该佩戴口罩充满了矛盾与困惑,唯恐引起他人紧张和不爽,或者更有甚者,招致种族主义攻击。美国社会为什么反对戴口罩?

NEW YORK—Krystal Ji, a China-born lawyer working in San Francisco's busy Financial District, believes that wearing face masks reduces her risk of contracting the new coronavirus. But a seemingly minor incident last week convinced the 26-year-old to ditch them.

Ji was waiting for the elevator in her company's lobby, wearing a mask. When the elevator came, a man behind her saw the mask and decided to wait for the next one, even though there was plenty of room.

"I was so embarrassed and became super self-conscious whenever I put my masks on," Ji told the *Nikkei Asian Review*. "Even though my bosses and colleagues never said anything about me wearing masks, I just thought I might make them feel uncomfortable."

Ji's experience hints at a fundamental difference in how masks are viewed in the West versus Asia. Many U.S. residents of Asian descent appear to be conflicted over whether to wear them—lest they make others nervous or, worse, invite racist attacks.

Public anxiety in the U.S. has grown alongside rising case numbers. Since the country confirmed its first infection in January, the tally has soared past 1300, with concentrations in the states of New York, Washington and California.

But while China, for one, insists that people wear masks in an attempt to limit community spread, U.S. officials have strongly advised against wearing them. This advice comes from the top—U.S. Surgeon General Jerome Adams—who has repeatedly said people should just wash their hands and avoid crowds.

"Seriously people—STOP BUYING MASKS!" Adams tweeted earlier this month. "They are NOT effective in preventing general public from catching Coronavirus, but if healthcare providers can't get them to care for sick patients, it puts them and our communities at risk!"

Likewise, the Centers for Disease Control and Prevention website say "the routine use of respirators outside of workplace settings" is not recommended among healthy individuals.

While American consumers have certainly bought their share of masks since the crisis started, not everyone is at ease wearing them in public. There are multiple reasons for this, "but I think the most important one is cultural," said Xi Chen, assistant professor of health policy and economics at the Yale School of Public Health.

"Traditionally, Western societies believe only those infected should wear face masks because they could spread the virus, but healthy people do not need to do so."

But the differences in policy are also "economic", Chen said.

Medical-grade masks are "definitely effective" in reducing the likelihood of infecting others as well as lowering one's own chances of infection, Chen said. But "if everybody needs one face mask every day, we would need at least 300 million. In the American market there is definitely no such supply".

Over 90% of the personal protective equipment used in the U. S. is made overseas, with China as the biggest supplier, according to the Department of Health and Human Services.

But since the coronavirus broke out, the Chinese government has directed factories to prioritize domestic demand. Hospitals across the U. S. are rationing their surgical mask supplies and only fit-tested health care workers can receive N95 respirators. Many U. S. state health departments have made their emergency mask stockpiles available.

Some doctors in the U. S. are also arguing that masks give wearers a false sense of security.

"Masks usually don't prevent you from catching disease," said Dr. Fred Davis, associate chair of Emergency Medicine at Northwell Health's Long Island Jewish Medical Center. "The standard is basically hand hygiene, which is cleaning your hands and washing your hands effectively. The problem is if you're not sick, having the mask on gives you that false sense that you're safe and then you forget to wash your hands."

"You keep that mask on all day, it gets wet and it just breeds its own site of infection," Davis continued.

Besides washing hands, U. S. experts stress the importance of keeping one's distance from others. The CDC notes that respiratory viruses spread from person-to-person through close contact, within 2 meters. Surgeon General Adams tweeted this week that people should "take everyday precautions to keep space between yourself and others" and "when you go out in public, keep away from others who are sick, limit close contact."

But Yale University's Chen—while conceding that the lower population density in the U. S. makes masks less of a must-have—draws a distinction between rural towns and large cities where maintaining distance is not always easy.

"I think they should say something more specific—in bigger cities, it makes sense to wear masks, especially for vulnerable groups," Chen said.

When New York City declared a mask shortage last week, Health Commissioner Oxiris Barbot said in a statement that "while we do not advise healthy New Yorkers wear masks, they do provide a public health benefit in some situations".

All this leaves Asian communities in the U. S. wondering what to believe and how to protect themselves.

"I think people should wear masks in New York because of the density of the population here and the lack of infrastructure for people to have access to sanitation," said a 25-year-old Chinese woman in the city, who asked not to be named. "But I won't wear masks because local authorities don't recommend wearing masks in public, and I've seen people wearing masks who got attacked. Wearing masks is not accepted by the culture here."

Some are haunted by concerns over hate crimes. There have been multiple reports of coronavirus-related public assaults on Asians—with and without masks.

On Tuesday, a teenager kicked a 59-year-old Asian man to the ground from the back and spat in his face in the Upper East Side of Manhattan, while yelling "F**king Chinese coronavirus," according to the *New York Post*. On the same day, a 23-year-old Asian woman was reportedly punched in the face by an acquaintance in the Midtown area. The suspect used racist slurs before fleeing, according to NBC News.

Rather than encouraging residents to cover up with masks, the state of New York introduced large-scale social distancing measures this week, banning gatherings exceeding 500 participants and ordering Broadway theaters to shut their doors.

Cassy Liu, a freelance writer in Los Angeles, disagrees with the common American perspective on masks.

"Not wearing masks just because you don't have any symptoms now makes no sense," she said, noting it can take 14 days for symptoms to appear. "Even if you are healthy, you need to consider others around you with weaker immune systems. You can easily infect others without even knowing that you had the virus."

Yale's Chen sees a danger of the American public underestimating the coronavirus and said it is vital to increase testing. For now, people who are infected may not fully understand their risk because of the shortage of test kits and the long incubation period.

"In an ideal world, if everyone knows for sure if they are infected or not, we can advise only the infected to wear masks," Chen said. "But now there are people on the streets who don't understand their risk, and this could put the population in danger."

(Marrian Zhou, Yifan Yu and Alex Fang, "Nikkei Staff Writers". *Https://asia. nikkei. com/Spotlight/Coronavirus/Asians-in-US-torn-between-safety-and-stigma-over-face-masks*)

Words and Expressions

tally	n.	记录，统计数据
respirator	n.	口罩，呼吸器，防毒面具
ration	vi. / vt.	定量配给
stockpile	n.	储存，储备
precaution	n.	预防措施
vulnerable	adj.	脆弱的，易受伤害的
sanitation	n.	卫生设施，公共卫生
assault	n. /vt.	攻击，殴打
slur	n.	诽谤，诋毁
freelance	n.	自由作家，自由职业者
immune	adj.	免疫的
	n.	免疫者
incubation	n.	潜伏期

（四）文化冲击/文化冲突

文化冲击（Culture Shock）是人们来到一个新的或陌生的社会文化环境中旅行、工作或生活时所体验到的不确定性、困惑或焦虑感。由于不同国家和地区的社会规范会有相当大的差异，一个人一旦进入新环境，对其习俗、语言和行为习惯不熟悉，就会产生文化冲击。

一般来说，文化冲击不是由某个特定事件引起的，而是当人们置身于一个新环境中，面对不同的做事方式，原有的价值观和行为模式受到质疑，原有的行为线索被切断，又不知道如何行事和应对，就会产生挫败、困惑、焦虑、孤独和不安等情绪。文化冲击还可能导致对新文化的排斥和敌对、失去耐心、抑郁等负面情绪和极端行为。

文化冲击一般会经历四个不同阶段：蜜月期、挫折期、调整期和接受期。虽然每个人经历这些阶段的方式不同，每个阶段的顺序和产生的影响也不相同，但是，对各阶段有清晰的认识对尽快适应和应对新文化很有帮助。

1. 蜜月期（Honeymoon Stage）

文化冲击的第一阶段通常是非常积极的。在这一阶段，人们通常会对新环境兴奋不已，并将其看作是一次冒险经历。如果是短期停留，这种最初的兴奋可能贯穿整个行程。然而，如果是长期定居于此，这个蜜月期最终会结束。

2. 挫折期（Frustration Stage）

遭受挫折可能是文化冲击中最困难的阶段。当新环境最初带来的喜悦逐渐消失，令人困惑和不舒服的情况不断出现。例如，对他人的行为、话语和习惯感到费解，误解不断，疲劳感随之而来。人们会发现当地的人和环境不再那么友好，这些情况可能会让他们觉得被冒犯或感到孤立，他们会变得越来越烦躁、迷失、想家。甚至一些细节问题也令人烦恼，例如下文提到的个人出行方式改变、公共交通的便利性。

"One thing that was particularly frustrating to me in the beginning was the lack of mobility that I experienced in the U. S. Where I grew up in Germany, you can get to any point at any time thanks to a great public transportation system, sidewalks and bike lanes everywhere. In the U. S., you are very limited in the things you can do if you don't have a car and I completely underestimated how much you have to depend on others to get around. I realized that home, for me, meant to live in a place with countless opportunities and absolute freedom. I felt less independent and I think that this was one of the main reasons I felt homesick (besides the obvious ones: family, friends, etc.)."—Arne Plum, business operations analyst

3. 调整期（Adjustment Stage）

当外来者开始对新环境的文化、人、食物和语言逐渐感到熟悉、适应时，他们的挫败感就会得到抑制，这时他们发现建立朋友圈和获得社区支持变得容易了，当地语言的细节也容易识别。这些变化都有利于他们自我调整，深入理解当地文化。

当然，在这个调整阶段，人们依然会遇到各种问题，但是他们能够理性、恰如其分地处理问题。例如下文提到的通过多询问、多了解，尽快适应新环境。

"Because I was in Turkey for six months in a study abroad setting, acclimating to my new environment was sped up due to all of the resources I was able to access. However, I found that the best way to understand my new environment was to ask questions and learn to respect the culture in the way it currently exists. The local Turkish people seemed much more accommodating when I showed genuine interest in their customs, rather than obviously being an American who was uncomfortable with her new situation. I also found myself asking my Turkish roommates what was okay to do, not okay to do, where to go and where not to go, so I was able to adjust to my environment more quickly."—Kate Riley, marketing and communications intern

4. 适应期（Adaptation Stage）

经过一段时间，可能是几周、几个月甚至几年，历经一番困惑与情感纠结之后，人们不再感到孤立无援，他们已经习惯了新环境，结交了朋友，进入适应或接受阶段（Acceptance Stage），又称双重文化阶段（Bicultural Stage）。

当然，这种适应或接受并不意味着完全理解新的文化或环境，而是意识到完全理解并非是在新环境中生存和发展的必要条件。他们已经融入了新环境，可以获得足够的资源，自如地应对新生活，他们已经获得了归属感。正如有人反思的那样，不断比较和对比新旧环境，区分优劣：

"There was a time when I realized that constantly comparing and contrasting everything would never allow me to be really happy here. Qualifying the differences worked both ways, and I felt torn between my life here and what used to be my life back in Germany. So I began to see the differences as what they are—just differences—without trying to rate them or use them to put one place over the other. Over time, I felt much more at ease with my life in the U.S., and I began to understand that these differences are what living abroad is all about."—Arne Plum

文化冲击是海外生活、工作的重要组成部分，接受现实并积极寻找应对方案才是明智之选。Lauren McCluskey 是具有专业资格认证的人力资源资深人士，在服务业和航空业为国际大品牌客户服务方面积累了丰富经验，她对如何克服文化冲击提出以下建议：

1. Remember that it's normal

Culture shock is not a sign that anything is wrong. It's part of the expatriate experience and eventually, you will be able to look back on this process with fond memories.

You've been given the opportunity to live in a different part of the world and experience different cultures and tradition—both the good and the bad are all part of the adventure.

2. Make your own space

Travelling light is good but leaving a space in your suitcase for a few luxuries that will help you to personalize your new home.

Your favorite cushion or a framed picture can make a big difference to your space and help you feel at home more quickly. Build yourself a safe haven that you can come back to when it all gets a bit too much.

3. Keep an open mind

One of the most effective ways of dealing with culture shock is to keep an open mind and welcome the surprising experiences as they arise.

Commit to saying yes as much as possible. Accept invitations to events, eat strange food, offer to help out a new friend, and discover your new home's cultures and traditions for yourself. Of course, you should also use common sense and be sure to stay safe, healthy and not push yourself too hard.

4. Explore

Try to avoid hiding away too much. Get out there and explore.

Feel free to live the tourist life. A great way of doing this is via public transport. Ride around the city with your camera or commit to visiting a new place every day, even if it's simply a quick turn down a new street on your way home.

You might even discover a faster route to get to work, find a new hangout where you can relax, or snap a fantastic photo to share with friends and family back home.

5. Find something you really love

Find something you love to do in your new home. It could be anything from wandering the museum, to sipping coffee in the park, or hiking the mountains. That way when things get difficult, you can go back to that experience or place to cheer you up and remind you why you came to this country in the first place.

6. Set yourself a project

Find yourself a project. Whether that be learning how to prepare a local dish, practicing the steps of traditional dance, or memorizing some useful phrases in the local language—keep yourself busy with something new and exciting.

Having a project to work on will give you a sense of achievement and prevent you from dwelling too much on your culture shock.

(*Https://www. now-health. com/en/blog/culture-shock-stages/*)

全球化时代，文化冲击无时不在，我们可以将处理文化冲击看作是一个丰富人生阅历、提高应对和解决问题的能力的过程。Case 3 到 Case 6 从不同侧面描述了职场上遭遇的种种文化冲击和应对策略。

Case 3

Should I Leave to Go Back to the Culture I Like to Work In?

I'm a few months into a new job with a big corporate firm. I came here after four years working for successful high-growth websites and startups. I was enticed by a very impressive pay package, but they also offered an interesting challenge. However, I'm feeling a lot of culture shock that isn't dissipating. Despite the work being interesting and challenging, there's a lot about how stuff gets done that is making me unhappy and is getting in the way of me doing the things the business needs to succeed: there's a lot more bureaucracy than I'm used to working with; people care about hierarchies in a way that I'm not accustomed to; different teams seem very siloed; and it takes months to get access to basic software and tools that are industry standard.

There is support from senior management to change to a more "agile" (a wonky term, but it is a working practice) tech/startup/get-stuff-done/entrepreneurial approach, and the desire to change the culture is one of the reasons they hired me. But while I can encourage and champion change, it's not in my remit to make it happen and I don't think I'll win friends if I keep trying to get established practices to change.

I'm thinking of just chalking it up to being a bad cultural fit and leaving at the end of my probation. I specialize in the booming fintech industry and won't struggle to get another job. But I'm worried this will burn bridges, be the coward's way out, and could look bad on my CV (i. e. , like I was fired). I'm also concerned about Brexit and think it might be wiser to ride out 2019 in a large firm that could weather market shocks. So should I rough it out for a year and see if things improve? Or leave to go back to the culture I like to work in?

(*Https*: //www. theguardian. com/lifeandstyle/2018/oct/30/corporation-culture-shock-startups-work-problem*)

Words and Expressions

entice	*vt.*	诱惑，引诱
dissipating	*adj.*	驱散的，消散的
bureaucracy	*n.*	官僚作风
silo	*vt.*	孤立，把……储存在筒仓内
agile	*adj.*	（动作）敏捷的，灵活的
wonky	*adj.*	靠不住的，动摇的
champion	*vt.*	拥护，捍卫，支持
remit	*n.*	职权范围
chalk…up		归咎于，记下，达到
cultural fit		文化契合度，文化适应性
probation	*n.*	试用期，见习期
fintech (financial technology)	*n.*	金融科技
Brexit		英国脱欧
weather	*vt.*	平安渡过（困境），经受风吹雨打
rough out		对……做粗加工，勉强应付一下

Case 4

How to Deal with Culture Shock in Your Workplace

Culture shock is the reaction of surprise and confusion that many people experience when confronted with new social rules or standards. This applies to working abroad as much as moving between companies. When working in a new company you may be shocked or confused by some of the unwritten rules of workplace etiquette. Do colleagues expect you to respond to emails outside of work time, or maybe you are surprised to find your colleagues resistant to answer your after-hours queries? Does your CEO maintain distance between lower employees or are you having lunch with her? Do people take long lunches with a glass of wine, or squeeze lunch into thirty minutes?

Often these unwritten or explicit rules are determined by the culture of the country or region you are working in, and if you are new to that environment, feelings of anxiety might be compounded further.

How can you deal with those moments that clash with what you are used to, and maybe even more importantly how do you avoid a cultural faux pas?

The key is simple. Avoid assumptions and ask questions. The first thing you must realize is that there is almost never one way to do anything. What is "normal" is not necessarily "best". However, if you can bravely ask questions about what is normal for your colleagues, then you will avoid making assumptions that could put you in an embarrassing situation, plus it will make it easier to build relationships with your colleagues by showing that you want to get to know them.

My personal experience is as an American living in Stockholm, working in a company with over 15 nationalities represented. The advantage of my work environment is that culture shock is not shocking. We all expect to find ourselves in a place where we are surprised by what is normal for our coworkers, which means that my colleagues are empathetic to my situation. However, it also means that we are a team that does not have a naturally aligned work culture.

What has saved me in the end is that I try to approach everything with an open mind. Maybe because we are a Swedish company, our organization is very flat, and this really surprised me. It often means that I am asked to be part of a process of consensus building before beginning work on a new project. I have had moments where I feel that being told to do something would be more efficient than a discussion about what to do. What I have realized however, is that by striving to reach consensus, everyone feels more involved in the company, more excited by company activities, and more willing to do something that they don't love, because they were approached for their opinion before the work was started. I have asked superiors and colleagues about how to appropriately contribute in this flat structure, and that has helped me be a better team member.

In the end, if we are okay to suffer the small embarrassment of asking a question that might make us look silly, it will save us the larger embarrassment of doing something that offends our colleagues. People will always respect you for trying to be a part of the group, but they might hate you if you ignore the established culture of a new workplace.

(Https://advice.milkround.com/deal-culture-shock-workplace)

Words and Expressions

compound	vt.	加重，恶化
faux pas	n.	（法）失礼，失态
empathetic	adj.	感同身受的
align	vt.	调整，使一致
consensus	n.	一致看法，共识

Case 5

Culture Shock in a British Workplace

This semester, I have been working as an editorial intern at Cultureshock Media in London. Cultureshock is a company that specializes in both print and online publishing, and their clients typically pertain to culture such as museums, music venues, or fashion companies. The first half of my semester in the United Kingdom was spent taking classes, but as soon as November came, my schedule shifted into working three full days out of the week. Since then I have worked with clients like British Airways, the British Council, and Sotheby's magazine. I've written newsletter and magazine content, researched cultural events, and created posts for Cultureshock's art review website (http://www.culturecritic.co.uk). As someone who wants to go into the publishing industry, this internship felt like the perfect placement.

Still, there were challenges in the beginning as I adjusted to a British workplace. Although everyone speaks English, it still might be hard to interpret what someone really means. If you'll excuse the wordplay, I definitely experienced culture shock at Cultureshock.

I've narrowed my experience to a few aspects that stood out the most to me—both because I wasn't expecting them and because they're so prominent.

Food and Drink: Both are very important in British culture. It's often a topic of conversation and is essential to bonding. First, if someone asks if you want the last biscuit, you say no. By asking other people in this manner, the person is actually saying that they want it. Knowing this helped me understand their politeness and roundabout way of asking for things, which would definitely help me later. More stereotypically, the British love tea. Instead of the clichéd "interns fetching coffee", you should anticipate learning how to make tea. Whenever someone gets up to make a hot drink, they are expected to ask everyone else if they'd like something as well. Both food and drink come into play at the pub, where the entire office might head on Friday nights. This is a great place to get to know your coworkers on a friendly level and ends up strengthening your working relationship as well.

Office Layout: I've been at Cultureshock for a few weeks and I'm still confused as to the company's hierarchy. This is because the office has an open layout. In a British office, the CEO could be sitting next to an intern, and everyone mingles with each other casually. Our office is an old apartment building, so aside from a separation between upstairs and downstairs, there aren't any divisions between departments. Making it even harder to differentiate hierarchy, British offices tend to be very young. Age doesn't necessarily denote seniority.

Receiving Direction: If your supervisor casually suggests you do something by saying "Oh, you might see if you can work on this before tomorrow" or "perhaps it would be a good idea to work on this before tomorrow", it actually means you need to do it before tomorrow. Similar to the indirect way of asking for the biscuit, the British don't tend to give specific direction. It is up to the employee to interpret what they want and manage their time well enough to get it done.

Writing: Surprisingly, writing hasn't been that different. The biggest thing I've come across is spelling. In British English, many words with an "or" at the end have a "u" in it, such as humour, rumour, or colour. Also, words with the suffix in "ize" or "izing" are spelled with an "s", such as traumatising or capitalise. Working with culture, I personally need to remember theater is spelled theatre over here.

These are only a few of the cultural aspects of an international workplace. Although seemingly random, understanding each helped me understand my coworkers better and thus get more out of my internship. By building a relationship through food and drink, I felt more comfortable asking questions to people I wouldn't have spoken with otherwise. They then became more willing to share some of their expertise with me. The open office also helped foster relationship building and department integration. I am lucky enough to sit next to my supervisor so if I am ever in need of specific direction, I can ask her face-to-face. Furthermore, I've been able to improve my communication skills by learning how to interpret her indirectness. Overall, it's been interesting to see both the differences and the similarities.

(By mbryant. Https://blogs.elon.edu/cupid/2015/03/12/culture-shock-in-the-workplace/)

Case 6

Professional Culture Shock

The biggest fear new recruits often report is that they don't live up to the linguistic or skills expectations that they may have raised in the job interview. And what often takes people aback is the inevitable clash between their own national and workplace culture and the new working environment.

Company vs. Country Culture

More than two thirds of adult employees recognize the importance of adapting to their company's environment in order to succeed in the organization, according to Randstad, the world's second largest HR service provider. But it's not always easy to see where the separation lies between company culture and the native national culture. Your mind will be doing overtime trying to figure out the rules by constantly observing and listening to the social codes; as well as trying to get on with your new job.

So the first rule is that in those early months, despite wanting to make the best impression and work your socks off, make sure you allow your poor psyche regular downtime from this double cultural adaptation process and exercise patience. It will serve you well in the long term.

One of my absolute favorite books on this subject is *Cultural Intelligence* by Brooks Peterson, because he directly addresses our psyche's need to go into a binary "my way" and "their way" thinking.

An example. In some cultures, asking questions is seen as an expression of being a responsible and "eager to learn" employee; even some recruitment companies advise you to ask a lot of questions at the start to make a good impression. However, in other cultures this is not seen as being positive, curious and willing to learn, but as a sign that you are not able to cope, or even as being rude and questioning the authority of your managers. If you find yourself being pushed from pillar to post because no one gives you a clear answer, then you may be in a national, or a company culture where no one owns responsibility for mistakes unless they are put in a senior position. And then hierarchy dictates that they are always right. As Peterson suggests, it is helpful to do a bit of research about the national culture that you have become part of and remember that, say, a Japanese company in Luxembourg may be more Japanese in its "hidden rules" than European. Peterson also comments that much of our own and others' cultural behaviors are unconscious, which means that a well-intended question or reflection on "is this how you all behave here?" can be genuinely misunderstood. So don't be afraid to announce the fact that you are a newcomer and a foreigner and that you fully expect to be putting your foot in it occasionally. If you can laugh about it, others will too.

Relationships with Your Co-workers

How you build relationships with your co-workers is an important step in the process of settling in. I have found that for most people it has served them to keep a bit of a low profile at first and observe the social codes. In your enthusiasm to please, you may not notice how your own cultural conditioning doesn't fit with how "we do things" here. One of my clients told me, "I came from New York with a very American 'shooting the breeze' kind of approach when I first started working here, but I seemed to meet a lot of resistance."

Another sore point may be that new colleagues aren't always forthcoming in including newcomers in their lunches or after work engagements. Others hoped that they would have had more help settling in, but have instead been left to their own devices. But perhaps these colleagues are just reluctant to intrude on your privacy; it might not be that they're not inviting YOU as a person, they're just letting time do the hard work for them and suddenly one day you'll find yourself heading out of the door with them at lunchtime, without any explicit invitations ever being issued.

Be patient, and avoid falling into the "everybody hates me" trap and then start acting like they already do. They don't.

They're probably just checking you out and having their own internal cultural adjustment process. This even happens in multi-cultural companies, where you would think everyone might meld into a unified global identity.

Timing Is Everything

National recruiters generally advise clients to expect things to be tough for the first three months. With international recruitment, I would extend that to anywhere from six months to a year. Remember, first impressions often only tell us something about the superficial layer of the new culture, so it's probably wise to wait a few months before judging your new situation too harshly.

New colleagues and managers seldom want to be compared to previous colleagues or managers, especially if you add a cultural twist. If you find yourself wanting to suggest they try and do things more like "we do in Holland" or "we do in Canada", you have gotten caught in what Peterson calls the "the hummingbird versus the turtle" dilemma and you are bound to get some resistance. Of course, it's natural for us to compare one with the other, and your insight may be very valuable. But save them until you find who would be sympathetic to your ideas, or when asked for an assessment by your managers.

Internal Combustion

Inevitably there will, at some point, be a conflict between the "old you" and the "new you", usually in the second half of your first international assignment year. Your psyche has been watching and observing, trying out to figure out the conscious and the unconscious codes, both corporate and cultural and you have been adjusting to these insights as best you can. We do so much to make the right impression from the start.

And there will also have been some time for your mind to begin to miss the "mirrors" from home that tell us who we are and how we should act. While being in a new environment is an excellent opportunity to have new aspects of ourselves mirrored back, we sometimes just need to be seen for who we know ourselves to be best.

When a colleague of mine said "well done Lysanne" in Dutch, six months into my first foreign job in London, I immediately burst into tears. It felt like a much needed homegrown slice of appreciation.

The most wonderful and the most challenging psychological aspect of living and working away from your own culture is that you don't need to become a different you, but that there can become more of you. My American client now says "I can be both 'American' in my way of meeting clients and colleagues, and be proud of that, but I also know when to melt into the background and be more like the locals. I am freer to be who I am, because I adjust, not to please others, but to help me perform better. The choice is mine."

So enjoy the adventure of your new international workplace. Don't be too eager to have it all together within the first few weeks, try to distinguish between the new culture, in and outside of your new workplace; and sit on your comparisons for a while until you've seen the underlying motivations behind surface behavior. Most importantly, don't lose who you are in the process; see your new situation as an opportunity to let go of parts of yourself that are no longer useful, and to embrace the new parts your host culture has helped find.

(By Lysanne Sizoo. *Http://www.healthyneurotics.com/professional-culture-shock/*)

Words and Expressions

work your socks off		拼命干活，拼命工作
downtime	*n.*	停工期，休息时间
binary	*adj.*	二元的
from pillar to post		从一处到另一处，从一个困难到另一个困难
put one's foot in it		失言；犯错误；因处理不当而招惹麻烦
to keep a bit of a low profile		保持低调
shooting the breeze		随便闲聊
dilemma	*n.*	进退两难，左右为难

第三章　如何提高跨文化交际能力

一、跨文化交际能力

跨文化交际能力是指与来自其他文化背景的人们进行有效沟通从而达到相互理解与合作的能力。跨文化交际能力（Intercultural Communication Competence）是一套认知、情感、行为技能和特征，是实现在不同文化背景下进行有效和恰当的沟通互动的能力（Intercultural competence is a set of cognitive, affective, and behavioral skills and characteristics that support effective and appropriate interaction in a variety of cultural contexts. —J. M. Bennett, 2013）。文化是通过交流习得的。人们在交流的同时也向他人展示个人的文化身份，人类通过交流创造和表达文化（Culture is learned through communication, and in turn, reveals the individual's cultural identity to others. Humans both create and express culture by communicating. —J. M. Bennett, 2013）。

有效的跨文化交际不仅需要娴熟的语言沟通能力，而且还需要具有跨文化意识，理解不同文化有不同的标准和规范，理解每个人都是由其生长的文化环境塑造的。每个人都是基于自己的文化认知来解读他人的文化，一个人所处的文化环境及其价值观决定了他的决策方式及其与他人互动的方式。因此，任何信息或决定所要表达的意义与被解读的意义可能不尽相同，由此产生的误解与不信任等负面效应更多是由文化差异造成的。

例如，在某些文化中，新入职的员工提问题被视为责任心强，是好学上进的表现；而在另一些文化中，则可能被视为工作能力和适应性差，或者是挑战上级权威的表现。又如，突出个人成就和自信满满的竞争力可能与集体主义的文化环境格格不入，在这种文化中，集体共享、顾及他人感受和相互依赖才是行为规范。

特别是在跨文化的团队环境中，文化差异的影响是巨大的。例如，当团队成员发现一个可能危及项目成功的问题时，许多美国人希望他们能直言不讳；而在其他许多文化中，这是不可能实现的，团队成员会认为发现这些问题应该是领导者的责任，他们不会提出问题，因为害怕惹怒领导，使领导失去面子，或者破坏团队的和谐。因此，提高跨文化交际能力首先需要处理文化差异带来的问题,加深对于不同文化模式、价值观和行为的认知有助于使自己的行为举止适应不同文化的非语言暗示、沟通互动方式、思维方式、冲突方式和价值观差异。

Case 1

Three Situations Where Cross-Cultural Communication Breaks Down

[提示]

本文陈述了来自不同文化背景的团队成员在头脑风暴、面对分歧、意见反馈中的种种表现与差异,并提供了解决方案。

The strength of cross-cultural teams is their diversity of experience, perspective, and insight. But to capture those riches, colleagues must commit to open communication; they must dare to share. Unfortunately, this is rarely easy. In the 25 years we've spent researching global work groups, we've found that challenges typically arise in three areas.

1. Eliciting Ideas

Participation norms differ greatly across cultures. Team members from more egalitarian and individualistic countries, such as the U.S. or Australia, may be accustomed to voicing their unfiltered opinions and ideas, while those from more hierarchical cultures, such as Japan, tend to speak up only after more senior colleagues have expressed their views. People from some cultures may hesitate to contribute because they worry about coming across as superficial or foolish; Finns, for example, favor a "think before you speak" approach, in stark contrast to the "shoot from the hip" attitude that is more prevalent among Americans.

Communication patterns may also make it difficult for people to participate equally in brainstorming sessions. Brazilians, for instance, are typically at ease with overlapping conversations and interruptions, viewing them as signs of engagement. But others, accustomed to more orderly patterns of communication, can feel cut off or crowded out by the same behavior.

The fix:

To ensure everyone is contributing, leaders of cross-cultural teams should establish clear communication protocols. A classic tactic, when soliciting ideas or opinions, is to go around the table (or conference line/video chat screens) at least once so that everyone has a chance to speak. Encourage exploration by asking open-ended questions and keeping your own thoughts to yourself at first. Recent research on teams of Americans and East Asians shows that such tactics result in dramatically more even contributions: Instead of taking five times as many opportunities to speak and using nearly 10 times as many words as their Chinese, Japanese, Korean, or Taiwanese colleagues, Americans took just 50% more turns and spoke just 4% more words when an inclusive team leadership approach was used.

If equitable air-time or interruptions are the problem, try adopting a "four-sentence rule" to limit your most loquacious team members, or insisting on an obligatory gap between two people's comments, to give everyone time to respectfully jump in.

2. Surfacing Disagreement

Comfort with public disagreement is another big source of conflict on cross-cultural teams. Members from cultures that place a high value on "face" and group harmony may be averse to confrontation because they assume it will descend into conflict and upset group dynamics—in short, social failure. In other cultures, having a "good fight" is actually a sign of trust. People from different parts of the world also vary in the amount of emotion they show, and expect from others, during a professional debate.

When, for example, people from Latin and Middle Eastern cultures raise their voices, colleagues from more neutral cultures can overestimate the degree of opposition being stated. On the flip side, when people from Asia or Scandinavia use silence and unreceptive body language to convey opposition, the message is often lost on more emotionally expressive peers.

The fix:

To encourage healthy debate, consider designating a devil's advocate whose remit is to consider and prompt discussion of the challenges associated with different propositions. The role can be rotated across agenda items or across meetings, so everyone becomes more comfortable in it. Another option is to spread the same responsibility by asking everyone to offer pros and cons on a particular course of action so people feel free to argue both sides, without getting locked in to positions they feel obliged to defend.

3. Giving Feedback

Constructive criticism is an essential part of global teamwork; it helps to iron out some of the inevitable kinks—relating to punctuality, communication style, or behavior in meetings—that aggravate stereotypes and disrupt collaboration. But feedback can be its own cultural minefield. Executives from more individualistic and task-oriented cultures, notably the U.S., are conditioned to see it as an opportunity for personal development; a "gift" best delivered and received immediately even if it's in front of the group. By contrast, people from more collectivist and relationship-oriented cultures may be unaccustomed to voicing or listening to criticism in public, even if the team would benefit. For face-saving reasons, they may prefer to meet one-on-one in an informal setting, possibly over lunch or outside the workplace.

If they come from hierarchical cultures, such as Malaysia or Mexico, they may not even feel it is their role to offer direct feedback to peers and instead deliver it to the team leader to convey. The words people choose to use will vary greatly too. Executives from low-context cultures, such as the Netherlands, for example, tend to be very direct in their corrective feedback, while those from high-context cultures, such as India or the Middle Eastern countries, often favor more nuanced language.

The fix:

Leaders should encourage members of cross-cultural teams to find a middle ground. You might coach people to soften critical feedback through positive framing and/or by addressing the whole team even when sending a message to just one person. For example, if time-keeping is a recurrent issue, you might say "I always appreciate it when we're all synchronized and we can make the most of our time together". It's also important to model the right behavior and show that you expect and appreciate constructive criticism yourself. A good starter question is: "Reviewing our meeting, what should I do more of, less of, and the same of?"

Beyond these quick fixes, teams need to pre-empt conflict on cross-cultural teams by developing a climate of trust where colleagues always feel safe to speak their minds. If you discuss potential problem areas early and often, you'll be well on your way to leveraging your group's diversity, instead of seeing your progress and performance stalled by it.

(By Ginka Toegel and Jean-Louis Barsoux. *Harvard Business Rewiew*. June 8, 2016)

Words & Expressions

perspective	n.	态度；观点
elicit	vt.	引起；引出
egalitarian	adj.	平等主义的
	n.	平等主义者
superficial	adj.	粗略的；肤浅的
shoot from the hip		信口开河；鲁莽地做事
overlap	vi.	重叠
protocol	n.	礼仪；外交礼节
tactic	n.	策略；手段
solicit	vt.	征求；索求；请求
loquacious	adj.	话多的；健谈的
obligatory	adj.	强制性的
confrontation	n.	对抗；对峙；冲突
neutral	adj.	中立的；中性的
overestimate	vt.	高估
on the flip side		另一方面
Scandinavia	n.	斯堪的纳维亚人
peer	n.	同龄人；同辈
proposition	n.	主张；观点；命题；建议
pros and cons		正反两方面；利弊；优缺点
iron out		解决，消除
kink	n.	问题；折裂；纽结
punctuality	n.	准时；严守时间
aggravate	vt.	加重；激怒
stereotype	n.	刻板印象；模式化观念（或形象）
nuanced	adj.	微妙的；有细微差别的
synchronize	vt.	（使）同步，在时间上一致，同速进行
pre-empt	vt.	预先制止，抢先一步
leverage	vt.	充分利用（资源、观点等）

Case 2

Six Fundamental Patterns of Cultural Differences

[提示]

本文展示了不同文化背景的人在沟通方式、面对冲突的态度、建立人际关系、完成任务的方式、决策方式、情感表达、认知方式方面的差异。

In a world as complex as ours, each of us is shaped by many factors, and culture is one of the powerful forces that acts on us. Anthropologists Kevin Avruch and Peter Black explain the importance of culture this way:

...One's own culture provides the "lens" through which we view the world; the "logic"... by which we order it; the "grammar"... by which it makes sense.

In other words, culture is central to what we see, how we make sense of what we see, and how we express ourselves.

As people from different cultural groups take on the exciting challenge of working together, cultural values sometimes conflict. We can misunderstand each other, and react in ways that can hinder what are otherwise promising partnerships. Oftentimes, we aren't aware that culture is acting upon us. Sometimes, we are not even aware that we have cultural values or assumptions that are different from others'.

1. Different Communication Styles

The way people communicate varies widely between, and even within, cultures. One aspect of communication style is language usage. Across cultures, some words and phrases are used in different ways. For example, even in countries that share the English language, the meaning of "yes" varies from "maybe, I'll consider it" to "definitely so" with many shades in between.

Another major aspect of communication style is the degree of importance given to non-verbal communication. Non-verbal communication includes not only facial expressions and gestures; it also involves seating arrangements, personal distance, and sense of time. In addition, different norms regarding the appropriate degree of assertiveness in communicating can add to cultural misunderstandings. For instance, some white Americans typically consider raised voices to be a sign that a fight has begun, while some black, Jewish and Italian Americans often feel that an increase in volume is a sign of an exciting conversation among friends. Thus, some white Americans may react with greater alarm to a loud discussion than would members of some American ethnic or non-white racial groups.

2. Different Attitudes Toward Conflict

Some cultures view conflict as a positive thing, while others view it as something to be avoided. In the U.S., conflict is not usually desirable; but people often are encouraged to deal directly with conflicts that do arise. In fact, face-to-face meetings customarily are recommended as the way to work through whatever problems exist. In contrast, in many Eastern countries, open conflict is experienced as embarrassing or demeaning; as a rule, differences are best worked out quietly. A written exchange might be the favored means to address the conflict.

3. Different Approaches to Completing Tasks

From culture to culture, there are different ways that people move toward completing tasks. Some reasons include different access to resources, different judgments of the rewards associated with task completion, different notions of time, and varied ideas about how relationship-building and task-oriented work should go together.

When it comes to working together effectively on a task, cultures differ with respect to the importance placed on establishing relationships early on in the collaboration. A case in point, Asian and Hispanic cultures tend to attach more value to developing relationships at the beginning of a shared project and more emphasis on task completion toward the end as compared with European-Americans. European-Americans tend to focus immediately on the task at hand, and let relationships develop as they work on the task. This does not mean that people from any one of these cultural backgrounds are more or less committed to accomplishing the task, or value relationships more or less; it means they may pursue them differently.

4. Different Decision-Making Styles

The roles individuals play in decision-making vary widely from culture to culture. For example, in the U.S., decisions are frequently delegated—that is, an official assigns responsibility for a particular matter to a subordinate. In many Southern European and Latin American countries, there is a strong value placed on holding decision-making responsibilities oneself. When decisions are made by groups of people, majority rule is a common approach in the U.S.; in Japan consensus is the preferred mode. Be aware that individuals' expectations about their own roles in shaping a decision may be influenced by their cultural frame of reference.

5. Different Attitudes Toward Disclosure

In some cultures, it is not appropriate to be frank about emotions, about the reasons behind a conflict or a misunderstanding, or about personal information. Keep this in mind when you are in a dialogue or when you are working with others. When you are dealing with a conflict, be mindful that people may differ in what they feel comfortable revealing. Questions that may seem natural to you—What was the conflict about? What was your role in the conflict? What was the sequence of events? —may seem intrusive to others. The variation among cultures in attitudes toward disclosure is also something to consider before you conclude that you have an accurate reading of the views, experiences, and goals of the people with whom you are working.

6. Different Approaches to Knowing

Notable differences occur among cultural groups when it comes to epistemologies—that is, the ways people come to know things. European cultures tend to consider information acquired through cognitive means, such as counting and measuring, more valid than other ways of coming to know things. Compare that to African cultures' preference for affective ways of knowing, including symbolic imagery and rhythm. Asian cultures' epistemologies tend to emphasize the validity of knowledge gained through striving toward transcendence.

Recent popular works demonstrate that our own society is paying more attention to previously overlooked ways of knowing. Indeed, these different approaches to knowing could affect ways of analyzing a community problem or finding ways to resolve it. Some members of your group may want to do library research to understand a shared problem better and identify possible solutions. Others may prefer to visit places and people who have experienced challenges like the ones you are facing, and get a feeling for what has worked elsewhere.

(Marcelle E. DuPraw and Marya Axner, "Working on Common Cross-cultural Communication Challenges". *Https://www.pbs.org/ampu/crosscult.html*)

Words & Expressions

anthropologist	*n.*	人类学家
assumption	*n.*	假定；假设
assertiveness	*n.*	自信；魄力
ethnic	*adj.*	民族的；种族的

demeaning	*adj.*	降低身份的；失去尊严的
notion	*n.*	概念；观念
Hispanic	*adj.*	西班牙的；西班牙语国家（尤指拉丁美洲）的
delegate	*vt.*	授（权）；把（工作、权力等）委托（给下级）
subordinate	*n.*	下属；下级；部属
disclosure	*n.*	披露；公开；揭露
intrusive	*adj.*	冒犯；侵入的；闯入的
epistemology	*n.*	认识论
transcendence	*n.*	超越

Case 3

Nothing Works Better than a Little Competition?

[提示]

美国人相信，适当的竞争可以提高业绩。这家美国公司让其位于日本和以色列的分公司展开相互竞争，但为何这一策略以失败而告终？

An American senior program manager was looking for the fastest way to develop a key product targeting an attractive emerging market segment. His primary product development resources were located in the United States, Israel, and Japan. Convinced that "nothing works better than a little competition", he commissioned both the Israeli and Japanese teams to independently develop a similar product. Each was to collaborate with the American side. The winner, the first team to create a viable product, would "take it all". Potential market returns more than warranted the investment, especially since the executive believed the approach would significantly reduce precious time to market.

What happened then: neither team did particularly well. The Japanese side procrastinated, going through several loops of questioning and clarifying. They generally seemed to give the project low priority. The Israelis complained a lot and suffered from low team morale, with a few key players even leaving the company. The project was a failure. It took major efforts, including redefining the structure and relaunching the project, to ultimately get a product out of the door. That product was late to market and struggled to compete with other solutions.

What happened here?

The executive manager ignored one of the most important principles of international project work: the need to understand one's own values and those of the other culture(s) involved. Setting up two teams to compete with each other internally might work well in the American work environment, where competitiveness is often highly valued and people go to great lengths to win. In Israel and Japan, as well as in many other cultures, the approach sent a very different message to the teams: that their competence was not being trusted. Accordingly, their motivation was low and they didn't put in their best efforts. Predictably, each team reacted in ways typical of their culture. The end result was the same for both of them: not much got accomplished.

International project work, especially in cross-cultural co-development settings where teams collaborate and compete simultaneously, requires special skills. Effective project leaders strike a careful balance between the various values and preferences of each of the (domestic and foreign) cultures involved.

(*Http://www.leadershipcrossroads.com/arti_ipl.asp*)

Words & Expressions

viable	*adj.*	可行的；可实施的
procrastinate	*vi.*	拖延；耽搁
simultaneously	*adv.*	同时；急切地

二、跨文化交际能力的构成

跨文化交际能力由多种要素构成，主要包括动机、了解自身文化和其他文化，以及对不确定性的容忍度等。

1. 动机

一个人的内在或外在动机使得跨文化交流成为一种自愿的、有回报的、终身学习的过程。当然，处于主导地位的群体对跨文化交流的意愿和动机要比其他群体弱，会有意无意地期待其他群体来适应自己的文化。在这种不平衡的交际环境中，来自非主导群体的个人需要更多地表现出其适应对方文化的能力和态度。例如，为了确保海外业务与投资的安全和获益，外来投资者必须积极主动地去适应当地的商业习惯与规则。

美国强生公司亚太研发与创新人力资源负责人李梦涓女士指出：跨文化沟通最重要的是要学会"Seek first to understand, then to be understood."。我们要带着好奇心去了解别人的文化背景及其建立信任的沟通方式，因为建立信任的方式在不同文化背景中可能会存在差异。

2. 对不确定性的容忍度

跨文化交际常常会带来不确定性。在与不同性别、种族或国籍的人交流时，人们想要知道自己应该做什么，不能做什么，应该说什么，不能说什么。对不确定性的容忍度是指个人在不确定的情况下对不确定情况的态度和感觉的舒适度。研究表明，对不确定性容忍度高的人可能会表现出更多的耐心，愿意积极寻求更多信息，这样可以更深入地了解情况，从而取得想要的结果；而对不确定性容忍度低的人在跨文化交际中感受到的焦虑可能会使他/她逃避交流或者交流不畅。同时，跨文化交际动机强的人对不确定性的容忍度更高。

3. 知己知彼

文化差异对国际交往和跨国经营的影响不容忽视，涉及语言、沟通方式、建立信任的方式、人才的评价标准、经营理念、价值观等诸多方面。

例如，中西方都崇尚诚实守信和彬彬有礼，但是西方人把诚实守信放在第一位，而传统上，中国人则更看重忠诚、面子和礼节；中国人视谦虚谨慎为美德，而西方人更看重的是自信心和决策能力；西方人每日"谢谢"不离口，哪怕最亲密的人之间也不例外，而在中国，亲朋好友之间频繁道谢会让人觉得不舒服，还可能预示着相互关系正在疏远。

特别是，文化差异会导致人与人之间缺乏信任，因为信任本身具有不同的意义。摩托罗拉公司一位负责全球组织发展的副总裁说："人们对信任的观念很不一样。在中国，人们因你的名位而信任你，你是老板，你的员工自然对你信任。但是在美国，人们对你的信任来自你的所作所为，而不是你名片上的头衔、社会关系、经济地位。"然而，"在我们这个人际关系至关重要的社会，信任是关系深厚的结果；深厚的关系或者来源于长久的直接交往，或者来自可信任的、间接的关系。面对完全陌生的异国人文环境、薄弱的人际关系，抱着我们固有的信任观不放是危险的"。

要想实现有效的跨文化沟通，我们首先需要了解自己，了解自己的文化、思维方式、价值观和沟通方式，这些我们习以为常但又往往忽视的文化特征时刻影响着我们的跨文化交流与沟通。如果我们想要传递的信息与他人接收到的信息相左，那就意味着我们的沟通出现了问题，我们对不同文化之间的差异理解不透彻。

了解自身文化和其他文化最有效的途径是与来自不同文化的群体进行交流沟通，这需要走出自己的舒适区域，倾听来自不同文化的观点理念，从而发现自己的自我认知与他人的看法有着天壤之别。例如，有的瑞典学生对来自美国的学生始终保持一定的社交距离，因为在他们看来，美国人看似热情友好，但是友情不能长久，一旦离开便不再是朋友。这让他们意识到两种文化在交往方式上的差异，瑞典人通常比美国人保守，需要更长时间建立友情，而美国人性格相对外向，这让一些瑞典人高估了他们之间的关系，最终，当美国人不再保持联系时，他们备感受到伤害。

然而，由于种种条件的限制，人们可能并不那么容易获得与来自不同文化的人直接打交道的机会。那么，学习另一种语言也是了解另一种文化的有效途径，这样就可以直接用这种语言阅读原文信息，观看视频，避免翻译中丢失信息可能带来的麻烦，因为，掌握另一种语言并不等同于掌握了跨文化交际能力。Case 4、Case 5 和 Case 6 展现了工作场景中的东西文化差异。

Case 4

Major Corporate Cultural Differences Between Western and Eastern Workplaces

[提示]

本文揭示的中西方企业文化差异主要表现在：员工之间的相处之道、员工与企业的相互关系、批评的意义与方式、时间观念、提问的意义与方式、如何面对上级或权威等。

1. Relationships

In the West, people tend to prefer formal meetings in which to engage in business activities, close relationships with each other. That said, the occasional office get-together provides the opportunity to bond through any mutual embarrassment that may ensue.

In terms of the employee's relationships with the company they work for, Western societies have lesser expectations as to whether corporations take care of their workers (beyond what is required by law). The majority of Westerners likely wouldn't be surprised by a company terminating their contract as a result of poor performance. Similarly, employees have no issue leaving their current employment to greener pastures if the opportunity comes up.

In the East, instead of keeping relationships strictly professional, personal sharing and the development of closer long-term bonds is favored and encouraged. There is a desire to form relationships with colleagues, something which requires time and trust to create, and individuals can often feel offended or shamed if others do not reciprocate. Efforts to develop these relationships are commonplace. In Japan, for example, activities such as karaoke are a perfect example of after-work engagement between colleagues.

In comparison to the West, corporate Asia tends to be less strict on hiring from the outset, and is generally more lenient to any under-performers on staff. Employees are loyal to their employers, and there is a societal expectation that employers will take care of their employees. People don't wish to work with strangers, and they don't form relationships easily. That said, when a relationship has been established, it can often last for a lifetime.

2. Criticism

What constitutes criticism—or where the line between advice, expert opinion, or seniority is even located—can be very different depending on the cultural work context you're enveloped by. In the West, calling people out on their mistakes is pretty standard. In fact, it's often seen as an important part of developing a strong and effective team. Tackling problems head-on and letting colleagues know about their shortfalls or errors is totally acceptable, though the way you do so may vary between territories. A snarky joke about a problem might be an effective approach in the UK, but it may be seen as offensive in Germany, where people might prefer to receive only the bare facts related to their error and nothing more. Similarly, a polite email would do the job in the US. No matter the approach, the fact is, in the West problems are flagged and fingers are pointed at those responsible. Furthermore, the related anger, frustration, and other applicable emotions may be on display.

In the East, criticizing a workmate in front of other members of the team is practically unthinkable. People will try to avoid these sorts of situations as much as possible. In fact, if there's any way to do away with unpleasant circumstances altogether, this is the preferred route to take. In China, for example, the concept of "saving face" sits at the core of the culture. Criticism is reserved for private interactions, and is often delivered through a third party. "Face" is a tricky thing to get your head around, and if you're heading to China we recommend you research far deeper into the subject.

In general, populations in the East are more reserved and don't readily expose their emotions. Maintaining harmony and avoiding conflict is considered an essential aspiration to uphold.

3. Punctuality

Being on time for work or work-related engagements is a big part of corporate culture in both the East and the West. Nobody likes to wait around for someone else to arrive and it's generally considered rude and unprofessional to be tardy. Time is money etc. and there's nothing fashionable about being late when business is concerned. Still, there are a few potential complications that you ought to be aware of.

In the West, local norms can be challenging even between Westerners of different origins. Though people try to arrive at a designated time and start meetings without much delay, it's become more and more commonplace to adhere to "flexible hours". In this context, as long as the work gets done, and meetings are attended, no problem. The expectation is simply that other team members are reliable. Furthermore, if someone proves not reliable, they'll soon be called out on it!

Nevertheless, if you've agreed to meet a Spaniard at 10 am, they might not arrive until 11am (though they likely understood that you already knew this would be the case when you arranged the meeting). Germans will arrive early. So a meeting between the two, without assurances of the rules being followed, can be a frustrating affair.

Even time—and how it's treated—differs from Western to Eastern workplaces.

In fact, many other "common understandings" related to meeting times exist throughout a variety of European regions. "The academic quarter", for example, is the 15 minutes discrepancy between the official start time of a university lecture and the actual starting time. Essentially, learn the local rules and play by them.

In the East, punctuality isn't quite as clear cut in the Eastern cultures. The higher and more powerful a person's position is, the less important it is that they are prompt. It is totally acceptable for management to be late to a meeting, but less so for workers with lower ranks. Nevertheless, arriving late to the office or to a meeting in Asia may well pass without comment. There is an assumption that you had a good reason, so expect to be queried on what that reason was once the meeting is over.

Additionally, meetings in the East might begin with some unofficial socializing and "warming up" between those in attendance. As we discovered earlier, relationships are important in Eastern business cultures, so diving straight in would be considered a bit odd.

4. Questions

The simple act of asking a question can be received in many different ways by the person being asked, as well as by onlookers.

In the West, asking questions is regarded as standard practice; in fact it's expected that lower-ranking employees show their initiative by seeking to expand their understanding of key topics by asking about them. Employees are encouraged to ask questions, even if these may be challenging to the ideas and actions of their superiors. It's not that, as an employee, you are necessarily challenging ideas, but rather simply trying to get your head around them and understand motives and processes better. Employers value this sort of thing, as it shows that the individual asking the questions is eager to learn more in order to become a bigger asset to the company. Leaders in the West, after all, are just another member of the team.

In the East, things work differently. Employees would likely feel intimidated by the idea of asking questions. There is a fear that superiors might see questions as threatening, since they would have to clarify their position on a given subject. Far more emphasis is given to the importance of politeness and not openly discussing opinions, disagreements, or pointing out flaws. Leadership in the East is just that, and should not be questioned. We will discuss this further in the final section, below.

5. Authority

Hierarchy is something you will encounter in any workplace. The severity of that system of status and authority, however, may differ greatly between locations and territories.

In the West, hierarchies tend to be relatively flat. You should feel comfortable talking to your manager, and even the CEO of a company, without issue. Chances are you can even call them by their first name. People in higher positions will generally try to help their subordinates feel that there is a sense of equality amongst the team (on the surface, at least). Each person's opinion is valid, and all ideas are welcome. Final decisions are based on the team's input, and nobody agrees with anything simply for the sake of it—there is a shared belief that that's not how problems get solved. Potential issues should be flagged as early as possible and reconsidered, regardless of the status of the person raising the point. Furthermore, criticism of employees in front of each other is commonplace. You're just hashing out ideas, so it's probably fine to shut down un-constructive input.

In the East, the hierarchical system has many more levels, and each level really means something. Those at the top have the final word, and the system of order and governance is considered to be extremely important. Seniority genuinely matters. For example, interns in Singapore often note that Chinese values of *guanxi* (relationships) and hierarchies are common—people seldom violate chains of command or openly question decisions by their superiors.

From the manner (and order) that each person is greeted, served drinks (for example), or interacted with, it's all based on position and authority. Managers will rarely scold their staff or people associated with their business in front of others, and any suggestions or input will likely be made with subtle inferences and non-verbal clues particular to their country or region therein. Eastern managers often consider themselves as secondary father figures to their employees, something which harks back to the long-term relationships and established bonds we discussed earlier.

(By Dickon Stone. *Https://www.goabroad.com/articles/intern-abroad/east-vs-west-corporate-cultural-differences-for-interns-abroad*)

Words & Expressions

terminate	*vi.*	终止；结束
reciprocate	*v.*	回应；回报
lenient	*adj.*	宽大的，宽容的，仁慈的
snarky	*adj.*	尖锐批评的；讽刺挖苦的
aspiration	*n.*	渴望；抱负；志向
tardy	*adj.*	迟缓的；迟到的
discrepancy	*n.*	差异；不符合
query	*vt.*	询问；怀疑；提问
intimidate	*vt.*	胁迫；使害怕
flaw	*n.*	缺陷；瑕疵
hash	*vt.*	反复推敲；仔细考虑
subtle	*adj.*	不易察觉的；微妙的
hark back		回到本题，重提，回想

Case 5

East vs. West: Cultural Differences in the Workplace

[提示]

本文描述了日本企业与美国企业的工作环境、做事方式、员工与企业以及员工之间的相处模式。

I will share some cultural differences I have noticed based on my personal experience working in American and Japanese companies.

Horizontal & Vertical Work Environment

One of the things that floored me when I first entered as an intern for a Japanese company was the work space. My jobs in America, aside from the freelance part, often featured separate spaces for each member of the staff. Even when I worked at gyms, there was a designated room for each supervisor, human resources, front desk, and trainers. It made stopping by various stations to ask questions or make contact rather awkward and difficult. Plus, it always felt like management was separated from the overall energy of the workplace; but when that door opened to reveal the superior's space, it never seemed to be for a good reason. In other words, the chain of command was clearly defined by where people worked, how big their space was, and so on.

That said, some work environments in Western cultures are very horizontal.

In Japan, however, though certain departments might be separated by a wall, the management is usually in the same space you are. This makes it very easy to pick up your laptop, walk over to their desk, ask for a minute, and receive immediate feedback. It also increases the amount of productivity throughout the office, because you can easily communicate with everyone present. Whenever announcements had to be made, you simply send around an email then call it. I quite like the level of comfort that people have within this setting. We're all on the same playing field, in a sense.

Types of Feedback

In many Western workplaces, when you make a mistake, feedback is often provided right then and there. Or, you are called into the office and given either positive or negative criticism on how you are doing. Usually, the manager tries to be as level-headed as possible and provide constructive criticism so you can improve. Training is designed to ensure you make mistakes then, not when you've been hired for several months then encounter a problem and have no means of correcting or mitigating it until your boss finds out and guts you for it.

Japan, as well as other eastern countries like China, is all about saving face. While it is recognized that people make mistakes and sometimes need negative feedback to improve on their skills, you will rarely be told to your face that you messed up. Rather, you will be told in private or not told at all. For example, a coworker of mine repeatedly showed up late to work one month. Instead of the boss going to him about it and asking why he was tardy all the time, they made an announcement during a meeting about certain people needing to develop better time management skills. Though sometimes, you are removed from a project for a reason that doesn't have to do with the mistake you made, simply because the superior or person in charge doesn't want to be the bearer of bad news.

It's kind of up to you to read the nuances in conversation and note whether the critique deals with something you did or not.

Meetings & Conversations

This is where the lines begin to blur. Meetings are usually the same wherever you go, I've found. There is usually an opening greeting from the person leading the discussion, ideas are shared, and then other announcements are made that pertain to everyone in the room. However, it is the matter in which this news is communicated that is different.

English speakers, as well as some other western languages, do not have variations in how you speak to someone, regardless of where they stand on the social ladder. Japan, on the other hand, has a system called "keigo". This refers to the amount of respect your words carry when speaking to an individual or group whom is either beneath you or above you in the workplace. For example, I wouldn't speak to the CEO in the same way I would a high school student. If I did, I'd probably be fired.

The same applies to when you speak with customers. In America, for example, while you may take on a slightly politer tone, there are no grammatical points that alter the level of respect your show towards said customer. In Japan, you again apply the rules of "keigo".

The other difference between Eastern and Western business would be the Japanese concept of「飛び込み営業」which has to deal with visiting companies without making an appointment. For a person to approach a company to sell a service or product without setting up a meeting time in many Western countries is unthinkable. You would be turned away immediately. Turns out, making cold-calls and visiting locations randomly is slightly less of a nuisance in Japan.

Company Relationships

The biggest difference between the East and West workplace would be the relationships you form with your boss and coworkers. I know that when I worked in America, while friendships would form at work, being treated like family, in a sense, didn't really happen unless you've been with the same coworkers for years on end. There were no real company trips. Hardly any parties. And people were forbidden from dating one another, because that usually leads to unwanted drama.

When I first arrived in the Japanese workplace as an intern, I immediately felt like I was dropped in the middle of a J-drama. People were laughing together, going to the convenience store, talking about going on dates, inviting people drinking, and even the CEO offered to take me to a bar as a welcome. Up to now, we've had welcome parties, gone on company trips to onsen (Japanese hot springs), and even have had coworkers dating one another.

Openly Networking

The last major difference I wanted to touch on was how professionals keep in touch and share their information. Though social media has become something of an electronic business card for many Western cultures, Japan still relies heavily on the paper or plastic version. These are handed out whenever you meet someone new or when the information has been updated. Business cards, known as "名刺" or "meishi" in Japan, are essential to establishing a means of contact with another individual. If you want to be seen as professional, you are going to need to apply this practice. That's not to say things like Facebook, LinkedIn, and other sites aren't beneficial, because they are. But the business card continues to reign supreme in business-making traditions.

There are many more differences between East and West workplaces to discuss, but many of them are based off of these main dissimilarities. Overall, it is the culture of the country that is reflected in the work space. Where the West is a bit more loose and casual in terms of how they operate, Japan continues to be a little more rigid with their proceedings and formalities.

(By Valerie Taylor. March 9, 2018. *Https://talenthub.jp/blog/working-in-japan/east-vs-west-cultural-differences/*)

Words & Expressions

bearer	n.	传达消息者；送信人
nuance	n.	细微差别
critique	n.	评论文章；评论
blur	vi.	看不清楚；记不清
pertain to		属于；关于；适合
cold-call		陌生电话

Case 6

How to Impart Chinese Way of Communication to Dutch Employees

[提示]

本文描述了中国企业海外分公司外籍员工与总公司业务部门在沟通中遇到的问题。

In the Netherlands, it might be very normal that one's colleagues and friends are completely different groups of people. However, in the Chinese context, personal intimacy is expected within the working relationship. In the same light, purely work-related requests sometimes need to be formulated in a way of personal favor.

The case below was about giving a cheaper price to a customer, but this business request was interpreted as "asking for a favor" between the subsidiary and a department of the parent company. Since it is easier to settle something with an acquaintance, according to the Chinese norm, good personal relationships with internal business collaborators are crucial to fulfil business tasks.

A Chinese manager leads a team of Dutch employees who need to collaborate with different domestic departments of the parent company. He talked about his experience of imparting Chinese ways of communication to his Dutch employees.

Once, a Dutch employee complained "I have sent five emails in three consecutive days to a certain department of the parent company, but nobody has replied". Right, surely there is nobody who will reply to you. For one thing, they may not know you. This is because you are not contacting each other in daily life. You only contact someone when you want to ask for help. In China, we say you are not sincere, right? Moreover, maybe the way you said it is not appropriate. This is also possible ... For instance, you want to apply for a special price for your customer. The normal price is 1000, but you want to ask for 950. This is asking for a favor. How should you say it? If you say directly "Hey, this cargo needs to be shipped at 950, otherwise our customer will not let us ship it", the other party does not want to hear it: "Who cares! It's just one container."

You have to approach it another way— you have to tell them that this is our long term customer. If you give him 950 this time, there might be more containers next time. So, your purpose will be achieved. However, the Dutch employees may not adopt the second method.

When asked when the two parties are both working for the collective interest of the parent company such a tension still exists, the Chinese expat manager answered, "Although it is for the collective interest of the company as a whole, there are differences between partial and collective interests. After all, we have to complete our work targets."

The basic principles the Chinese manager conveyed in the case above could be interpreted along three points. First, personal relationship can help tremendously even in internal business collaborations. Moreover, one has to formulate a request politely in such a way that one offers the superior position to the internal collaborator. Furthermore, there could be competition or even a conflict of interests among different departments of the parent company. If one does not know how to deal with things tactically, the subsidiary will be confronted with bureaucratic indifference.

(By Tianmu Hong, Frank Pieke and Trevor Stam, "Chinese Companies in the Netherlands". *Leiden Asia Centre Press. Report-Chinese-companies-in-the-Netherlands-2017-final-. pdf*)

Words & Expressions

intimacy	*n.*	亲密；密切；关系密切
formulate	*vt.*	制订；规划
subsidiary	*adj.*	辅助的；附带的

impart	vt.	传授；告知
consecutive	adj.	连续的；连续不断的
tactically	adv.	战术性地；战术上

三、如何培养和提高跨文化交际能力

培养跨文化交际能力是一个复杂的过程，涉及个人思维与观念的转变和多种知识技能的综合运用。培养文化敏感性和跨文化意识，充分了解自己必须面对或适应的文化、历史、价值观和沟通方式，深刻理解文化对语言和沟通方式的影响，才能在跨文化交际中恰如其分地运用交流沟通策略。例如，鉴于土耳其与希腊的历史恩怨，向其推介对方的旅游或美食需要审慎考虑。又如，北欧人性格直率，语言表达直截了当，他们的英语表达中缺少英国人常用的"Please""Thank you"等礼貌用语，这对英国人来说是一种冒犯。

1. 积极主动交流沟通

用美国强生公司亚太研发与创新人力资源负责人李梦涓女士的话来说就是："说出来，说起来。"（Speaking out and speaking up.）"不愿'说出来'和不会'说起来'应该是中国人才的通病。'说出来、说起来'似乎和我们'沉默是金''三思而行'或者'枪打出头鸟'的观念相违背。"

2. 简明扼要——主动适应对方的沟通方式

深刻理解文化对语言和沟通方式的影响，主动适应对方的沟通方式和习惯。出于不同的文化背景，汉英民族的思维与表达习惯各异。汉语叙事习惯由远及近，先陈述事实及原因，然后得出结论，结尾点题。而英语往往首先点明主题或观点，然后依据事实陈述论证，主题或观点具有明显的标志性。

正如李梦涓女士所述，简明扼要、切中要害的交流方式更符合西方人直截了当的沟通方式，而我们更习惯"先因为，后所以"的思维模式，沟通时常常是娓娓道来，层层铺垫，有时会让西方人搞不清楚我们到底想要表达什么观点。在跨文化的工作环境里，我们要建立更好的跨文化认知和提升相关的敏锐度，并有意识地根据利益相关者的文化背景调整自己的沟通方式。

因此，我们要不断提高自己适应不同文化环境的能力，不能总是期望别人来适应自己。这也包括当别人无意做了让你不悦的事情时，虽然你不必接受，但最好礼貌地解释为什么你难以接受，而不是心生怨气或逃避沟通。

3. 8个有助于提高跨文化交际能力的技巧

第一，提前收集对方的相关信息，特别是掌握几个他们的日常用语，这有利于表达与对方交流沟通的意愿。Nelson Mandela说过，如果你用他/她能听懂的语言与他/她交谈，他/她会记住你。如果你用他/她的语言与他/她交谈，你会走进他/她心里。

第二，向有相关经历的同事、朋友征询意见，观看电视节目和各种短视频是了解其他文化和社会行为规范与禁忌的有效途径。

第三，说话前要从对方的角度去考虑他/她会怎样理解你传递的信息。

第四，注意个人行为举止发出的非语言暗示。

第五，避免使用方言俚语。当想不出更恰当的语言表达时，可以借助图像画面传递信息。

第六，善于观察倾听，注意信息反馈，通过不断提问确保双方相互理解正确，避免误解。

第七，如果发现自己无意中冒犯了他人，有效的弥补方式是迅速道歉，坦承自己的无知，忽视自己的过失意味着进一步冒犯。

第八，经常回顾反思自己的跨文化经历有助于总结经验，快速适应跨文化环境。

此外，要有同理心，学会通过想象他人的立场观点来理解他人，有助于减少偏见、消除刻板印象和抛弃种族优越感。建立自我文化意识，掌握跨文化技能，可以促进双方相互适应，减少误解和负面看法。

Case 7

Five Secrets to Meaningful Intercultural Communication

1. Keep It Simple

Think in terms of your audience and speak to their understanding. Yes, you are communicating with humans of diverse origins.

We all wish to comprehend each other and find joy in discovering common ground between us. To make things easier for everyone, be clear in your speech (enunciation, diction, grammar) and your purpose.

Be wary of jargon and complex structures such as double negatives. This also applies to idioms, as these are highly contextual. Though fun to use in business language, even expressions like "from the get-go", "touch base", and "ballpark figure" can be confusing and distract from your main idea.

This is very important to keep in mind as some members of your audience may not be fluent speakers of your language.

Ultimately, the best kind of message is a clear message.

2. R-E-S-P-E-C-T

Aretha Franklin couldn't have said it better. When people feel respected, understood, and listened to, it builds a profound level of trust and esteem.

This is the foundation of positive, rewarding relationships, and ideally what you should aim to achieve for powerful communication in any setting.

It can be challenging in intercultural settings to know what is acceptable, let alone effective, in communication. Some people will respond well to more frank and direct language and approaches, whilst others may find this aggressive. With conscientious research and observation, this will likely become easier as you go.

Being mindful of others; paying attention to their customs; showing curiosity about their traditions; being open and receptive to their worldviews—these are habits of people who interact with others effectively and consciously.

3. Strike a Chord

Great leaders know that true communication is never one-sided or void of emotion. In fact, anything related to teams or groups requires collective effort, cooperation, and, ideally, mutual understanding.

"The essence of cross-cultural communication has more to do with releasing responses than with sending messages. It is more important to release the right response than to send the right message." —*Edward T. Hall*

With this in mind, consider how you view yourself in relation to others. Of course, if you are in a higher-tier (executive or managerial) role, you are responsible for others and perhaps not on their same level as far as the business' organization is concerned. However, your amount of authority and duty over others does not have to dictate your form of personal expression.

If you wish to really resonate with your team or audience, speak to them as equals and partners. Communicate in a way that not only carries but evokes emotion.

A great trick for leaving a deeper impression can be as simple as choosing your words wisely. Think about the difference between the words "lead" and "command", or "educate" and "enforce". Words carry meaning, and the vocabulary that you use when communicating should be in line with the values and messages that you wish to convey.

4. When in Doubt, Leave It Out

It is human nature to be wary of the unknown. But for some of us, curiosity (and even overconfidence) can tempt us to try and tackle things that we are perhaps not prepared for.

As strangers to another culture, we may only see and perceive what is already familiar to us, potentially misunderstanding or critiquing things that we are not fully informed about.

Discussing certain cultural, religious, and political situations can provoke bias or tension, distracting from your message. If you do find yourself out of your depth when faced with an audience or an issue that is unfamiliar to you, don't fret! Take a moment to reflect, and approach sensitive subjects with due care.

This is a great opportunity to research and expand your knowledge base further. Otherwise, by diving straight into the deep end and "winging it", you may risk offending others (or, at the very least, coming across as unprofessional).

You know what they say about assuming!

5. Enjoy the Experience

"*A people without the knowledge of their past history, origin and culture is like a tree without roots.*"—*Marcus Garvey*

Perspective and attitude can have an immense effect on the way that you interact with others. Ultimately, communicating with others should be a pleasure, not a chore. And this should show when you do it.

If you have set up your business in a new market or are hoping to expand your business overseas, for example, this is a wonderful test of your business savvy, ambitions, and awareness.

Furthermore, those who embrace the global and intercultural aspect of business and life consider it a privilege to be able to interact with people who have so many different viewpoints and backgrounds to offer.

Of course, these differences can create gaps between people, potentially presenting challenges that affect productivity and professional rapport. But if we are to prepare for a future of international business and exchange networks that know no bounds, these gaps must be bridged. And this is where intercultural communication plays a key role.

(Https://www.thepolyglotgroup.com/5-secrets-to-meaningful-intercultural-communication/)

Words & Expressions

enunciation	n.	清晰的发音；阐明；表明
diction	n.	措辞；用语
jargon	n.	行话；黑话；术语
from the get-go		从一开始
touch base		保持联络；接触
ballpark figure		近似数；大约估计
esteem	n.	尊重；自尊；敬重
strike a chord		引起共鸣；动人心弦
higher-tier		高等级的；高层次的
dictate	vt.	决定；命令；支配；口述
resonate	vt.	产生共鸣；共振
evoke	vt.	唤起；引起（感情、记忆或形象）
be wary of		留神；谨防；提防
tackle	vt.	解决；应付；处理（难题或局面）
critique	vt.	写评论；对……发表评论；评判
provoke	vt.	激起；引起；引发；
bias	n.	偏见；偏心
out of your depth		非你力所能及
fret	vt.	烦恼；烦躁；苦恼；焦虑不安
wing it		即兴表演；即兴发挥
chore	n.	杂活；累活；苦差事
savvy	n.	理解能力；洞察力；实际知识
privilege	n.	特权；荣幸；优惠待遇

Case 8

Who Is to Pay?

In January I attended a course on racism that bore the title "Fighting against racism in Switzerland" supported by the Swiss Government. The class presented a quite heterogeneous crowd, both ethnically and professionally. During the lunch break, which we spent in a nearby restaurant, I was sitting near a young man from Chad who had been living in Switzerland for several years already. When it was time to pay for our meals, this person paid for my beverage. Quite spontaneously, I reached for my wallet with the intention to pay him back but he declined to dismiss me with a brisk gesture that betrayed some kind of indignation from his part. Even if it was just a bottle of mineral water, it didn't feel right to let him pay for me.

This state of affairs made me feel awkward and strengthened my determination to pay him back; so during the coffee break I offered him a cappuccino but it was obvious by then that he was a little bit upset if not offended: I started to talk about this misunderstanding openly, in a very care-free manner, in order to shed some light on this communicative cul-de-sac. He told me that Europeans are a bit too cold and detached and shouldn't be so formal. I explained to him that I couldn't avoid feeling bad and the desire to pay him back stemmed from a natural social reflex, that translates into an exigency to be polite.

The fact that he was an immigrant certainly didn't help; this led me to question his financial situation: him paying for me had produced some kind of guilt in me at the time. Also my social background, or better my personal approach to situations in general, had produced a sense of awkwardness in me because we hadn't spoken that much prior to the incident and whereas I would normally accept this gesture from a friend or from a close acquaintance, I couldn't do the same with a perfect stranger. In describing this situation I am possibly understanding it better: the young man just wanted to show his sympathy and his gesture was just part of his desire to start a new friendship. I reacted following my social code and ended up misunderstanding the young man's intention.

In both incidents, the misunderstandings had probably to do with different dimensions as the psychological, the religious or the social dimension. Not really knowing either the Chinese nor the Chadese culture, my analyses were more of a psychological or emotional nature but I can imagine that both incidents had a lot to do with different interpretations of certain values: for example the different behavioral patterns that exist between women and men and between elderly and younger people. The young man from Chad was maybe hurt because I, being a woman, offered him a coffee, even if it was a sign of gratitude.

(From "Case Studies in Intercultural Communication". Https://www.mic.usi.ch/case-studies-intercultural-communication)

Words & Expressions

heterogeneous	*adj.*	由很多种类组成的；各种各样的
ethnically	*adv.*	种族的；种族上
Chad	*n.*	乍得（国家名）
beverage	*n.*	（除水以外的）饮料
spontaneously	*adv.*	自发；自动；自然地
betray	*vt.*	流露（情感或特性）；背叛，违背（信仰、原则等）；泄露（机密，信息）
indignation	*n.*	愤慨；愤怒；义愤
shed some light on		弄清楚
cul-de-sac	*n.*	死胡同；困境
detached	*adj.*	不带感情的；单独的
reflex	*n.*	本能反应
exigency	*n.*	紧急情况；急切需要

第四章 高语境文化与低语境文化

　　根据世界文化的多样性和主流交际方式的差异，美国人类学家霍尔（Edward T. Hall）将不同文化划分为高语境文化和低语境文化，从交际与感知的角度说明在不同文化环境中语言和语境在交际中的地位和作用，即在现实的人际交往中，交际双方所传递的信息主要是来自交际场合（语境）还是来自交际语言本身。高语境文化和低语境文化的划分区分了在交际过程中由语境和非话语所传递的隐性信息与由语言编码所传递的显性信息之别，显示了文化对人类生活的影响无处不在，包括自我表达方式、情感交流方式、思维方式、行为方式、解决问题方式等。高语境文化和低语境文化的形成有其深刻的历史文化根源。

一、高语境文化与低语境文化的形成

　　1. 高语境文化

　　高语境文化是人们在长期固定的交际环境中形成的。在这种文化环境中，人们生活的地域固定，社会生活变化缓慢，人们彼此间的交往是长期而稳定的，因而对生活环境有着相同的理解方式，形成了彼此认同的交际行为模式，交际双方在进行信息交流时对语言本身的依赖程度小，不必清晰地表达具体信息就能领会彼此的心意。

　　由于高语境文化受传统和历史的影响较大，形成了相对稳定的价值观、行为准则、民族心理等，人们彼此交流时，很多信息已经蕴含在背景信息之中，无须再用语言明确表达出来，完全可以意会，可以用表情、动作、眼神，甚至沉默等方式传递信息，双方通过交流环境就可以获取大量的信息内容，因此，高语境社会中，人与人之间的交流比较隐晦含蓄。

　　中国文化、日本文化、非洲文化、拉丁文化都属于高语境文化。这些地区的人们生活环境固定，社会生活变化缓慢，文化传统对现实生活的影响很大。

　　2. 低语境文化

　　与高语境文化不同，低语境文化的形成是比较孤立的。由于人们居住的地理区域比较松散，社会生活差异大，彼此间的交际比较独立，较少受到交际环境的影响，也就是说，交际环境本身和交流双方自身蕴含的信息量少，必须通过清晰明确的语言传递信息。

低语境社会大多出现在经济科技相对发达的国家和地区，社会成员流动性较大，文化传统变化较快，没有统一模式可依，人们很少依赖传统和习俗作为自己交流的准则或依据。例如，在欧美国家和地区，人们追求个人价值和自由，非常相信语言的感染力和说服力。美国人对演讲和辩论情有独钟，口齿伶俐，在美国，善于表达的人更容易成功。

3. 交际方式与思维方式的差异

高低语境的不同决定了身处其中的人们的交际方式和思维方式是不同的。如前文所述，高语境文化产生于相对稳定的历史文化传统之中，交流双方持有共同的风俗习惯、价值观和社会行为准则，交际环境足以传递充足的信息。例如，在中国这个高语境文化的环境中，语言不是传递信息的唯一途径，与交际相关的诸多因素如空间、沉默、手势、穿着、谈吐风格等都能给交际者传递所需信息，人们在交流中喜欢采用婉转隐晦的表达方式，较多考虑对方的感受，避免直接交流造成双方尴尬，而且，有些想法不可言传，只可意会。

低语境文化产生于独立、自由、个性化的社会环境之中，人们之间的交流对语境的依赖程度很低，在交流过程中注重事实依据和语言表达的逻辑性，喜欢直接坦率地表达自己的思想和观点，不善于根据语境去揣测对方的想法。

例如，在中国文化中，人与人的沟通讲究点到为止，心领神会。在工作场所，除了法规和行业规范，各行各业都普遍存在着诸多不言而喻的规矩礼俗需要遵守。而西方文化则相反，沟通方式直截了当，开门见山，信息表达明确无误，一般没有隐藏在字里行间的言外之意。工作场合照章办事，没有人情债，没有越规的例外。

因此，对于高语境文化的人来说，提高个人的敏感性与领会话外之音的能力，以及理解隐含意义的能力尤为重要。而低语境文化的人则通过诸如辩论和公共演讲等训练提高信息传播的效率和影响力。

一般来说，西方文化更依赖于低语境交流，这些国家包括澳大利亚、加拿大、新西兰、美国以及欧洲大部分地区。然而，高语境交流也时常发生在低语境文化中，例如，世界上几乎任何地方的家庭或关系密切的团体内部的交流都是高语境交流。同时，由于全球化的影响和东西方交往的实际需求，在高语境文化中，低语境交流变得越来越普遍，从网上购物到对外宣传，以及跨国商务谈判，都采用低语境交流，信息传递具体详尽。

高语境文化和低语境文化在思维方式上也有很大不同，在认知方式上表现为依存性与独立性的差异（如本章 Case 2 所述）。依存性是指依赖群体，把自己所在环境看成一个整体，自己只是其中的一分子。独立性则重视个人权力和竞争力，把部分和整体区别开来。例如，欧美国家强调个体化的独立性，而崇尚集体主义的中国则更偏重依存性，这就是为什么电子支付的生态易于在中国形成，而在欧美国家，电子支付则被视为对个人财富和隐私的侵犯。

在工作中，低语境文化的人常常将人与事分开，就事论事，强调的是工作关系，而不是人与人之间的关系，批评也是对事不对人，对一些非语言交际行为视而不见。相反，高语境文化的人往往将人与事联系在一起，批评某件事就等于批评某个人或某些人，人们有很强的保全面子的动机，说话婉转谨慎，认为保持社会和谐、避免冲突尤为重要。人们还具有很强的敏感性和信息捕捉能力，面部表情、交往速度、交往地点、难以言说的情绪、微妙的手势和声调以及周围环境细节等都是丰富的信息符号，传递着无限的信息与内涵。

Case 1

High and Low Context Communication

As a rule, cultures with western European roots rely more heavily on low-context communication. These include Australia, Canada, New Zealand, and the United States, as well as much of Europe. The rest of the world tends toward high-context communication. Naturally, high-context communication can occur in a low-context culture. Communication within a family or close-knit group is high context in almost any part of the world. Conversely, low-context communication is becoming more common in high-context cultures, due to Western influences and a desire to accommodate travelers and expatriates.

One of the more obvious markers of a low-context culture is the proliferation of signs and written instructions. If I step off the train in Munich, there are signs everywhere to direct me to the taxi stand, public transportation, ticket offices, tourist information, and lavatories. Detailed street maps of the area are mounted on the walls, and bus and tram schedules are posted. In much of the high-context world, there is little such information. Nonetheless everyone seems already to know where to go and what to do. Much of what one must know to operate is absorbed from the culture, as if by osmosis. In these parts of the world, my hosts normally send someone to meet me on the platform, partly as a gesture of hospitality, but also because they are accustomed to providing information through a social context rather than impersonal signs. I am much less likely to be greeted in a German airport or

第四章　高语境文化与低语境文化——交际方式与思维方式之别

station, not because Germans are inhospitable, but because they transmit information in a different way.

It may appear that low-context communication is simply an outgrowth of urbanization and international travel, rather than a cultural trait. These are certainly factors, but there is an irreducible cultural element as well. The smallest town in the United States carefully labels every street with a street sign and numbers the buildings consecutively, even though practically everyone in sight has lived there a lifetime and can name the occupants of every house. Yet very few streets in the huge city of Tokyo are labeled or even have names, and building numbers are nonexistent or arranged in random order. The United States and Japan are perhaps the world's most extreme cases of low-context and high-context cultures, respectively.

International travel and migration likewise fail to explain low-context and high-context behavior, even if they are factors. It is true that international airports are now well signed in most of the world. Yet there are few areas with a more transient and multicultural population than some of the Arab Gulf states, in which perhaps less than twenty percent of the population is indigenous. Communication nonetheless remains largely high context. Local authorities may post directional signs at roundabouts, in an effort to accommodate Western tourists and expatriates, but these are remarkably useless—no doubt because the local people never rely on signs and therefore do not really know what it means to navigate by them.

(John Hooker, "Cultural Differences in Business Communication". December 2008. Https://public.tepper.cmu.edu/jnh/businessCommunication.pdf)

Words & Expressions

close-knit	adj.	（由感情、利益、文化等）紧密结合在一起的；组织严密的
conversely	adv.	相反地
accommodate	vt.	给……提供方便；容纳；迎合
expatriate	n.	旅居国外者，侨民
proliferation	n.	激增；扩散
osmosis	n.	潜移默化；耳濡目染；渗透
impersonal	adj.	没有人情味的，冷淡的
irreducible	adj.	不能减弱的；不能减少的
occupant	n.	居住者；占有人

random	adj.	任意的，任意选取的
transient	adj.	临时的；暂住的
indigenous	adj.	本地的，土生土长的
roundabout	n.	环形交叉路口；绕行路线；绕道
navigate	vt.	领航，导航

Case 2

Cultural Differences in Business Communication

Communication is fundamental in business, because business is a collaborative activity. Goods and services are created and exchanged through the close coordination of many persons, sometimes within a single village, and sometimes across global distances. Coordination of this kind requires intense communication. Complex product specifications and production schedules must be mutually understood, and intricate deals between trading partners must be negotiated. Communication styles vary enormously around the world, and these contribute to a staggering variety of business styles.

Probably the single most useful concept for understanding cultural differences in business communication is Edward T. Hall's (1976) distinction of low-context and high-context cultures. It explains much about how negotiation proceeds, how agreements are specified, and how workers are managed. Yet this distinction, insightful as it is, is derivative. It is best understood as reflecting a more fundamental distinction between rule-based and relationship-based cultures, which is in turn grounded in different conceptions of human nature. The discussion here begins by showing how business practices reflect low-context and high-context characteristics, but it subsequently moves to the deeper levels to explore how communication styles are integrally related to other characteristics of the culture.

Regulating Behavior

Low- and high-context communication styles are, at root, contrasting approaches to regulating behavior. One way to identify a low-context culture is that behavior norms are often communicated by putting them in writing rather than through personal enforcement. If I am not supposed to enter a particular area or smoke there, posted signs will let me know. In a high-context culture, there may be no signs, but a guard or employee may accost me if I break any of the rules. I may take offense at this, because in a Western country, being called down for bad behavior implies that I should have known better, and I normally cannot know better unless someone writes down the rules. But in high-context cultures, being corrected by other persons is a normal procedure for regulating behavior.

Whereas Westerners live in a world of rules and instructions and are lost without them, many others live in a social context. A Western or international airport is full of signs and display screens that direct passengers to the correct check-in counter and gate, update departure times, and so forth. However, if I enter a crowded departure lounge in a regional, non-Western airport, I may find no signs or displays to indicate which gate corresponds to which destination, or if the displays exist, they may be blank or incorrect. Airline employees standing at the doorways may announce the flights, but they are inaudible in the din. Somehow, everyone knows where to go. They pick up cues from the people around them. For example, they may have unconsciously noticed who was in the queue with them when they checked in, and gravitated toward these same people when they reached the departure lounge.

There are clear implications for business communication. A manager in New York City transmits behavior norms through employee manuals and official memos. Employees who want a week off, for example, are expected to consult these sources, or perhaps their employment contracts, for whether they are entitled to a holiday. They follow prescribed procedures for filing a request, which is granted according to company policy. How employees make use of their holiday is of no consequence. In fact, managers typically want as little discretion as possible to evaluate the merits of the case, because they feel more comfortable applying rules than exercising personal judgment that they may have to defend. Employees in Bogotá, by contrast, will more likely approach the boss, or a friend of the boss who can plead their case. They will explain how important it is to attend a niece's wedding in Miami or grandfather's funeral in Buenos Aires. The boss is willing to make such decisions, because this is what it means to be a boss. Ironically, it may also be necessary to follow bureaucratic procedure that is even more tedious than in New York City, but the request is ultimately granted on the basis of personal decision. The role of bureaucracy in high-context cultures is an interesting issue and will be taken up later.

Because company norms in a high-context culture must be communicated personally, close personal supervision is essential. Rules that are not personally enforced may be seen as non-binding. The company may not want employees to use company cars for personal business, but a failure to monitor vehicle use may be interpreted as granting them permission. A similar principle applies in education. The instructor may tell students not to copy homework solutions from their classmates and state this policy clearly in the course syllabus. Yet if it is easy to copy solutions without getting caught, the students may feel free to do so. They reason that if the instructor really cared about copying, he or she would not allow it to occur.

Contracts

The difference between low- and high-context communication is particularly evident in the area of contracts. Western contracts are marvels of thoroughness. So simple a transaction as renting a bicycle for a day may require three pages of fine print to spell out how to deal with every possible contingency. Once a contract is signed, there is no flexibility in the terms unless both parties agree to renegotiate. If a party fails to deliver, the legal system is expected to enforce compliance.

Contracts in high-context societies have a different character, for two reasons. One reason traces directly to the high-context nature of communication. It is not necessary to write everything (or perhaps anything) down, because mutual understanding and a handshake suffice. When there is a written contract, it may be more a memorandum of understanding than a binding legal document. Because the terms are vague, there is room for adjustment as the situation develops. As for compliance, the parties are more likely to rely on a pre-existing trust relationship than a legal system.

A second reason for the lack of detailed contracts is that the very idea of a contract is central only in certain cultures, primarily those historically influenced by the Middle East. A Westerner, for example, sees doing business as synonymous with making deals. The idea of a covenant is fundamental to the culture and even governs the relationship between God and humankind in the Christian Old Testament. In a Confucian culture, by contrast, doing business is primarily about developing personal relationships. These can be based on family or clan connections, or on relationships of mutual obligation popularly known as guānxì (a Mandarin Chinese word for "connection"). Business plans develop along with the relationship rather than through formal communication in written contracts. Managers may draw up contracts to please their Western business partners, but one should not be surprised if they want to alter the terms the day after the document is signed. Why enslave oneself to a piece of paper, when the world constantly changes?

Negotiation and Decision Making

Every cross-cultural business manual cautions Western negotiators that, in much of the world, "yes" does not necessarily mean yes, and "maybe" can mean no. "Yes" can be a way of indicating that one understands or acknowledges a proposal. If the proposal is unsatisfactory, the response is likely to be indirect, perhaps consisting of such statements as, "we will think about it," a period of silence (as in a Japanese setting, where silence can have other meanings as well), or simply a failure to pursue the matter in subsequent meetings.

This kind of indirect speech relies on high-context communication to get the message across, but there is more involved than simply a tendency to engage in high-context communication. There is a desire to save face or otherwise avoid giving offense. Indirect speech occurs generally in situations where parties may disagree, not only in negotiation, but also when a decision is being discussed or conflicts must be resolved. Westerners tend to be frank in such settings. Parties who disagree state their views openly, because their differences are resolved by what are regarded as objective standards. The winning view is the one backed by the stronger argument, spreadsheet calculations, or the logic of market forces. The losers may find their predicament unpleasant, but they are expected to subjugate their personal feelings to objective criteria.

In much of the world, however, there is no such faith in objectivity. Life revolves around human relationships rather than what are seen as universal rules of logic. Because there is no independent standard by which to resolve conflicts, it is important not to give offense in the first place. Such scruples may not apply during transient interactions with strangers, as when bargaining in a street bazaar. But when dealing with business associates with whom one must maintain working relationships, it is necessary to preserve harmony through deference, courtesy, and indirection.

One result of this dynamic is that business meetings tend to serve different purposes in different parts of the world. In low-context cultures, meetings provide an occasion for the company to consider pros and cons and perhaps even arrive at a decision on the spot. Participants in the meeting are expected to express their opinions openly, provided they back up their views with facts and arguments. In high-context cultures, deliberation and decision-making tend to take place behind the scenes and at upper levels. A meeting might be an occasion to announce and explain the decision.

As for negotiation, the very concept, at least as it is understood in the West, may be problematic in a relationship-based culture. It may be seen as a form of confrontation that undermines harmony. Westerners view negotiation as a poker game in which players can lose without hard feelings, as long as everyone plays by rules that are somehow writ in the sky. Yet when no such rules are acknowledged, and only human relationships are recognized as real, it is best to foster these relationships and build trust. If there is common ground for business, it will develop along with the relationship.

Confrontational bargaining can be appropriate in high-context cultures, but again, only in such settings as a street market, and not between colleagues. High-context communication remains part of the picture, but it has a different purpose. The object is not to avoid giving offense but to arrive at a price with as little information exchange as possible. As a Westerner, I may regard "haggling" as a waste of time, because I believe the price should be dictated by the logic of the market. However, if there is no well defined market price, a price below my maximum and above the seller's minimum must somehow be arrived at. This is impossible if I reveal my maximum and the seller reveals her minimum, because I will insist buying at her minimum, and she will insist on selling at my maximum. Bargaining tends to be a ritualized activity that reveals just enough information about the seller and me to allow us to identify a price in this range, or discover that there is no mutually agreeable price. Hand and facial gestures, tone of voice, and walking out of the shop can signal intentions that are not explicit in verbal comments. Westerners often ask how they should bargain in a traditional market, but it is impossible to say in general. The conventions are very specific to the culture and must be learned over an extended period, perhaps by going to market with one's parents.

One-on-one bargaining of this kind can actually be more efficient, in an economic sense, than low-context Western commerce that explicitly reveals an equilibrated market price on a price tag or web site. Negotiation may discover a price on which the seller and I can agree, allowing mutually beneficial trade to proceed, even when one of us is dissatisfied with the market price and no trade would occur in a fixed-price system. In fact, some recent online auctions and trading are beginning to resemble traditional practices more than transparency-based Western commerce.

Relationship-based and Rule-based Cultures

This is a good point at which to examine the cultural mechanisms that underlie high- and low-context communication styles. They may be roughly categorized as relationship-based and rule-based. Each is associated with a suite of practices that regulate interpersonal relations and deal with the stress and uncertainty of human existence. This deeper perspective allows one to understand business communication patterns that are not fully explained as deriving from high- and low-context communication styles.

Behavior in relationship-based cultures is regulated through close supervision by authority figures. This requires that authority be respected, and it therefore resides in persons with whom one has significant relationships, such as parents, elders, bosses, or even departed ancestors. Improper behavior is deterred by shame, loss of face, punishment, or ostracism. Because the authority figures are close at hand and form an integral part of the social environment, behavioral norms are usually implicit in the cultural situation and need not be spelled out explicitly. Relationship-based cultures therefore tend to rely on high-context communication.

Behavior in rule-based cultures is based on respect for rules. This is not to say that rule-based cultures have rules and relationship-based cultures do not; both do. Rule-based cultures are distinguished by two characteristics: (a) people respect the rules for their own sake, while rules in relationship-based cultures derive their authority from the persons who lay them down; and (b) compliance with rules is often encouraged by guilt feelings and fear of punishment if one happens to be caught violating the rules, rather than shame and constant supervision. Because personal relationships are relatively unimportant in the enforcement of rules, the rules tend to be spelled out explicitly, and people are taught to pay attention to them. The result is low-context communication. One can now begin to see why high- and low-context communication styles are, at root, contrasting approaches to regulating behavior.

The distinction of relationship-based and rule-based cultures also underlies differences in negotiating styles. The frankness of rule-based cultures is possible because of an underlying confidence that rules have objective validity and can therefore serve as a basis for resolving disputes. The absence of such confidence in relationship-based cultures requires that they fall back on courtesy and face saving.

Relationship- and rule-based mechanisms deal with the stress and uncertainty of life as well as regulate behavior (Hooker, 2003). Family and friendship ties provide a sense of security in relationship-based societies. Loyalty obligations to family and cronies are therefore strong and may take precedence over one's own welfare, but it is loyalty well invested, because these institutions provide a refuge in difficult times.

The rule-based stress management mechanism is less obvious but equally fundamental to cultural success. Because social control does not rely so totally on personal relationships, these tend to weaken, and people must seek security and predictability elsewhere. Fortunately, the very rules that regulate behavior provide a basis for imposing order and predictability on society as a whole. The search for universality also leads to the discovery of scientific laws, which provide a basis for engineering the environment for even greater predictability and control. Rule-based peoples therefore turn as much to the system around them for security as to family and friends, or even more so. The systemic resources range from advanced medical technology to deal with disease to legal systems to resolve disputes.

(John Hooker, "Cultural Differences in Business Communication", December 2008. https://public.tepper.cmu.edu/jnh/businessCommunication.pdf)

Words & Expressions

specification	n.	说明书；规范
staggering	adj.	令人吃惊的；巨大的
insightful	adj.	富有洞察力的；有深刻见解的
derivative	adj.	被推论出的；衍生的
accost	vt.	（尤指唐突地）走近跟……讲话，跟……搭讪
correspond	vt.	相符合；相配，相称
inaudible	adj.	听不见的
gravitate	vt.	受吸引；移向（toward, to）
prescribe	vt.	规定，指定
discretion	n.	斟酌决定（或处理）权
tedious	adj.	冗长的，啰唆的；单调乏味的
transaction	n.	（一笔）交易；业务
contingency	n.	可能发生的事；偶然事件
compliance	n.	合规；遵从；依从
suffice	vt.	足够，满足要求
memorandum	n.	备忘录；纪要

binding	*adj.*	有约束力的；必须遵守的
synonymous	*adj.*	同义的
covenant	*n.*	契约，合同
enslave	*vt.*	使受控制（to）；奴役
spreadsheet	*n.*	电子表格；电子数据表
predicament	*n.*	处境；境况，情况
subjugate	*vt.*	使服从；压住；抑制
scruple	*n.*	顾虑，顾忌
bazaar	*n.*	（东方国家的）街市，市场；集市
dynamic	*n.*	动态；活力
pros and cons		有利有弊；赞成与反对；正面和反面
problematic	*adj.*	成问题的；有疑问的
undermine	*vt.*	逐渐损害（或削弱）；暗中破坏
foster	*vt.*	培养，促进，鼓励
haggling	*n.*	讨价还价；争论
ritualise	*vi./vt.*	仪式化；成惯例；使仪式化；使成惯例
equilibrate	*vt.*	使平衡；使保持平衡；与……平衡
auction	*n.*	拍卖
underlie	*vt.*	引起，使发生；构成……的基础（或起因）
deter	*vt.*	阻止，制止，防止
ostracism	*n.*	排斥
integral	*adj.*	构成整体所必需的；固有的；基本的；组成的
crony	*n.*	老朋友，密友
take precedence over		优于；（地位或重要程度上）高于

二、高语境和低语境折射的中美文化差异

1. 直接与间接

美国人习惯于坦率直白地表达自己的观点，注重自我表达和个人观点陈述，注重说服他人的能力。美国人面对或解决冲突与分歧时，常常列举大量事实，逻辑推理论证，具有一定的对抗性。而中国人则喜欢以间接的方式表达自

己的意愿，更多考虑对方的感受和面子，习惯于婉约其辞，把自己的想法迂回委婉地表达出来，避免言语上的咄咄逼人，避免出现尴尬局面。

但是，这两种文化下形成的不同的交际方式并无优劣之分。在全球化的今天，人们需要应对不同的交际环境和交际对象，需要恰如其分地运用相应的沟通与表达方式。例如，外交部发言人华春莹在 2020 年 4 月 11 日的一次答记者问中就采用了低语境文化的信息传播方式表达中国政府的立场，以线性逻辑推理的方式陈述事实和我方观点，说理论证过程无懈可击，对方无可辩驳（详见本章 Case 3）。

针对彭博社记者提出的"China's numbers were not real"和美国政客的指责，华春莹指出，"China has been giving open transparent and timely updates to the world"，然后依据 the daily information released by the Chinese government，从时间维度上举证说明，并由此做出反击："If the outbreak had hit the US first would it have handled the situation better than the Chinese government?"

对于病毒起源的质疑，华春莹引用了 WHO and experts on epidemiology and disease control 和 top academic journals 的观点，并提出建议直指问题要害："China invited WHO experts to visit Wuhan as part of a joint mission. As some in the US are so obsessed with the issue, we advise the US side to also invite WHO and international experts to visit the country and find the truth."这种直面问题的逻辑论证方式充分体现了论证说理全过程的客观性和真实性，事实依据环环相扣，语言表达明确无误，干净利落。

Case 3

Hua Chunying's Answer to Blooberg Reporter (April 11, 2020)

Q: The report concluded that China's numbers were not real. Do you have any comments on this?

A: As a Bloomberg reporter, you must be well aware of recent US media reports on the epidemic situation at home and the administration's response when you raised this question. I believe you already had an answer in your mind and just wanted to get it confirmed. I noted many US media's reports on what you mentioned US Vice President Pence and Secretary of State Pompeo said similar things on April 1 to accuse China of covering up the epidemic. They even claimed that China was dealing with the epidemic in December before the world learned about it. My colleagues and I have elaborating on all the details of China's response, which shows clearly that China has been giving open transparent and timely updates to the world. I believe you may have drawn the same conclusion based on the daily information released by the Chinese government.

On international public health security, we should listen to WHO and experts on epidemiology and disease control rather than several politicians who are habitual liars. In fact just yesterday a senior WHO official refuted unwarranted accusations on "China's untransparent data" in a press conference in Geneva. We sympathize with the US people as they are facing a severe situation and I can imagine why some in the US are trying so hard to shift the blame. We don't want to get into any meaningless argument with them.

But in response to their endless and immoral slanders, I feel I have no choice but to take a few moments to clarify the truth once again.

It is true that Wuhan was where COVID-19 cases were first reported. But where and when exactly did this virus originate? We read many recent reports and findings on that. There are articles written by medical professionals from Italy, the UK, the US, Australia and other countries, which are published in top academic journals including *Nature Medicine*.

On the origin of the virus, the Chinese government's position has been consistent. It is a serious matter that requires scientific, fact-based and professional assessment made by experts. Now there are various reports on experts' science-based and authoritative opinions. These views should be valued and respected by all including those politicians in the US.

China invited WHO experts to visit Wuhan as part of a joint mission. As some in the US are so obsessed with the issue, we advise the US side to also invite WHO and international experts to visit the country and find the truth.

The timeline of Chinese response is very clear, as you can gather from media reports.

On December 27, 2019, Zhang Ji-xian reported the first three suspected cases, director of the Department of Respiratory and Critical Care at Hubei Hospital of Integrated Traditional Chinese and Western Medicine.

On December 29, related centers for disease control and prevention and hospitals in Hubei and Wuhan carried out epidemiological investigation.

On December 30, Wuhan Municipal Health Committee issued an urgent notice on the treatment of pneumonia of unknown cause.

On December 31, the NHC sent an expert group to Wuhan to investigate on site.

China started to send timely updates to WHO and other countries including the US.

On January 8, the pathogen was preliminarily identified. The Chinese Center for Disease Control and Prevention uploaded five whole genome sequences of the novel coronavirus on website and shared data with the world and WHO.

On January 23, Wuhan was put under lockdown and unprecedented comprehensive thorough and rigorous measures were adopted.

By taking these decisive and strong measures, the Chinese government ensured to the highest possible extent the life and health of the Chinese people and bought precious time for stemming the global spread of the virus.

As I said yesterday, the journal *Science* published a paper by researchers in the United States, the UK and other countries, saying that China's control measure worked by successfully breaking the chain of transmission and bought other countries valuable time

Recently Dr Fauci, the medical expert leading the White House effort to contain the coronavirus reportedly said he refused to let others push him to say that China should warn the US three months beforehand, because it just doesn't comport with facts.

The *Lancet*'s editor said on BBC that "the message from China is very clear, we wasted February when we could have acted and it is a national scandal".

China has always been open, transparent and responsible in all its efforts. Can the few US individuals accusing China tell the world if the outbreak had hit the US first would it have handled the situation better than the Chinese government?

If their answer is yes I wonder if they could answer the following:

On January 15, the US CDC issued warnings on pneumonia caused by the coronavirus, the US announced the decision to close its consulate in Wuhan and withdraw all staff. On February 2, it banned entry of all Chinese nationals and foreign nationals who had been in China for the last 14 days. What has the US done in the two months since then?

According to a *New York Times* report on March 11, Dr Helen Y. Chu, a whistle-blower in the US, sounded the alarm on the epidemic in the US back in

January and reported her testing results to US regulators in February only to be told to "cease and desist" and "stop testing". At the end of February, the White House still asked officials and health experts to get approval from the office of Vice President Pence before making public statements on the epidemic. On March 2, the CDC stopped releasing data on tests and deaths. On March 2, Dr. McCarthy from the New York-Presbyterian Hospital said at a CNBC program that his hospital had to "plead" to health authorities to test suspected causes. Can they explain all this?

I've seen many reports calling on US officials to stop seeking excuses and scapegoats for their poor response. We understand the US is facing difficulties and some officials are under pressure and we feel deeply for the hardship of the American people.

Out of humanitarian spirit, we would like to provide support and help to them as our ability permits. However the comments by these few US politicians are just shameless and morally repulsive. As we have repeatedly said, slanders, smears and blame games cannot make up for lost time. More lies will only waste more time and lead to more lives lost. A word of advice to these politicians: at this moment, lives should come before politics. It is immoral and inhumane to politicize public health, which should be condemned by all in the US and beyond. I hope they will lose no more time and focus instead on fighting the pandemic and saving American lives.

I see you've been nodding in agreement. I hope you will help get my message across to the American people including the few individuals, who have been denigrating and smearing China. It would be much appreciated.

Words & Expressions

elaborate	vt.	详尽阐述
epidemiology	n.	流行病学
unwarranted	adj.	不确定的；无法证明为正当的
slander	n.	诽谤，诋毁；诽谤语
epidemiological	adj.	（疾病）流行性的
pneumonia	n.	肺炎
genome	n.	基因组，染色体组
sequence	n.	次序；顺序；连续；一连串
lockdown	n.	活动（或行动）限制
unprecedented	adj.	无前例的，空前的，前所未闻的；绝无仅有的

rigorous	adj.	严格的，严厉的；严峻的
stem	vt.	阻止；封堵；遏止
consulate	n.	领事馆
whistle-blower	n.	（尤指组织内部的）告发者；吹哨人
scapegoat	n.	代人受过的人；（喻）替罪羊
repulsive	adj.	令人厌恶的，可憎的；使人反感的
smear	vt./n.	诽谤，诋毁；弄脏
condemn	vt.	谴责
denigrate	vt.	诋毁，诽谤；贬低，轻视

2. 谈判策略上的明确详尽与模糊含蓄

跨文化谈判是指来自不同文化（即不同价值观，不同心理/思维方式，不同语言修辞等）的意欲交易、合作的双方，克服文化差异，充分运用跨文化理解力和沟通力，在双方约定的时间和地点，通过恰当与适量的信息交流方式和有效的沟通说服技巧，就特定的交易达成共识，最终满足各自需求的互动与博弈过程（贾文山，2019）。

商业谈判中，低语境文化的人趋向于线性逻辑思维，各项条款环环相扣，陈述明确详尽，面面俱到。而高语境文化的人通常使用较为"模糊含蓄"的表达方式，便于在交往的过程中作出判断和决策，随机应变，灵活机动。

中国文化的谈判观是先谈原则，使其成为控制谈判范围的框架。中国人"先谈原则，再谈细节"就是首先就涉及双方交易或合作的一般性问题交换意见，借此估计和试探对方，寻找和创造有利机会，达成有利于自身利益的条款或细节，将原则性协议转化为目标性协议，这样可以避免双方一开始就实质性问题和细节针锋相对，使谈判陷入僵局。

例如本章的 Case 4，中方声明体现了高语境传递信息的特征：只有少量信息通过语言或文字清晰传递，重点是创造"语境"而非"内容"，将建立相互信任看作实现商业利益的先决条件，追求建立长期的合作关系，然后再谈细节。语言表达概括含蓄，表明了谈判的积极意义。

西方的谈判观体现了一种竞争文化，谈判是一系列追求自身利益最大化的博弈。在西方世界，每个人都是一个独立的个体，人际关系并不具有法律约束力，只有契约条款才能将彼此的权力和义务划分清楚，保障双方的权益。

美方声明体现了低语境传递信息的特征：确定谈判的总体目标，按照线性逻辑思维的模式，详细规划谈判全过程，明确每个阶段需要解决的问题，一个问题接一个问题地谈，逐项达成协议条款，直至完成谈判全过程，形成一整套协议。语言表达直截了当，直白地提要求、谈条件，没有任何含糊其词、模棱两可的表述。

本章的 Case 4 是 2019 年 1 月 9 日中美贸易谈判的各自声明，一个是高语境的表述，另一个是低语境的表述，从双方各自的表述中可以窥见中美谈判策略的差异。属于集体主义文化的中国，特别注重维护谈判双方的和谐关系和面子，对待谈判中出现的冲突，中方采取的对策是暂时搁置，求同存异；而属于个人主义文化的美国，直面冲突，通过逐一落实合同条款，力图快速解决。

Case 4
Statements on the China-US Trade Meetings

中国商务部声明如下：

新华社 1 月 10 日消息：1 月 7 日至 9 日，中美双方在北京举行经贸问题副部级磋商。

双方积极落实两国元首重要共识，就共同关注的贸易问题和结构性问题进行了广泛、深入、细致的交流，增进了相互理解，为解决彼此关切问题奠定了基础。

双方同意继续保持密切联系。

美国贸易办公室声明如下：

美联社 1 月 9 日消息：1 月 9 日，美国贸易代表办公室发表声明，对刚刚在北京结束的美中贸易谈判作出情况说明。

声明指出："1 月 7 日至 9 日，由美国副贸易代表杰弗里·格里什（Jeffrey Gerrish）率领的美国官方代表团在北京与中国官员举行了会谈，讨论如何在两国贸易关系中实现公平、互惠和平衡。官员们还讨论了全面落实各项协议的必要性，对落实情况必须不断核查和有效地强制执行。此次会谈是唐纳德·特朗普总统和习近平主席在布宜诺斯艾利斯达成的共识的一部分，两位领导人同意在 90 天内谈判，以实现中国在强制技术转让、知识产权保护、非关税壁垒、网络攻击和出于商业目的的网络窃取商业机密、服务业、农业这些问题上必要的结构性转变。会谈还重点讨论了中国对于从美国购买大量农产品、能源、制成品以及其他产品和服务的承诺。美国官员转达了特朗普总统对于解决我们持续存在的贸易赤字和结构性问题以改善两国贸易的决心。"

声明表示，美国代表团将汇报会谈情况，以获得关于下一步行动的指导。

Statement on the United States Trade Delegation's Meetings in Beijing

January 9, 2019

On January 7 - 9, an official delegation from the United States led by Deputy U.S. Trade Representative Jeffrey Gerrish held meetings in Beijing with Chinese officials to discuss ways to achieve fairness, reciprocity, and balance in trade relations between our two countries. The officials also discussed the need for any agreement to provide for complete implementation subject to ongoing verification and effective enforcement. The meetings were held as part of the agreement reached by President Donald J. Trump and President Xi Jinping in Buenos Aires to engage in 90 days of negotiations with a view to achieving needed structural changes in China with respect to forced technology transfer, intellectual property protection, non-tariff barriers, cyber intrusions and cyber theft of trade secrets for commercial purposes, services, and agriculture. The talks also focused on China's pledge to purchase a substantial amount of agricultural, energy, manufactured goods, and other products and services from the United States. The United States officials conveyed President Trump's commitment to addressing our persistent trade deficit and to resolving structural issues in order to improve trade between our countries.

The delegation will now report back to receive guidance on the next steps.

Words & Expressions

reciprocity	*n.*	互惠，对等
implementation	*n.*	贯彻，执行；实施
verification	*n.*	证实；核实；查清
enforcement	*n.*	实施；强制执行
pledge	*n.*	保证，诺言；誓言
deficit	*n.*	逆差；赤字

三、高语境文化在中国企业海外投资中的具体表现

中国人含蓄模糊、灵活机动、随机应变的沟通与思维模式，以及边干边想、在沟通相处过程中判断决策的行为方式，同样也体现在中国企业的海外投资运作过程之中。根据荷兰莱顿大学亚洲研究中心（Leiden Asia Centre）对中国企业投资荷兰的调查报告——Chinese Companies in the Netherlands，中国文化的这些特征充分显现，如本章的 Case 5 所述。

Case 5

Main Obstacles Chinese Companies Face in the Initial Stages of Business Operations

In this chapter, we will focus on the main obstacles Chinese companies face during the initial stages of their business operations. How quickly they adjust to the new situation and deal with any difficulties that come their way, depends on the overseas experience of both the manager and the parent company.

1. Business plans

Many Chinese companies that come to the Netherlands do not have specific business development plans. They may have a general idea about what they want to do, but there seems to be a general lack of actual planning. Chinese companies believe that although business plans might be highly desirable, they should forge ahead even without well-researched plans.

Many Chinese companies operate according to the principle of "the front asking for ammunition." This means that the subsidiary leads the way, while the parent company provides support and follows. The same holds for making future plans. In one case, when asked what her company's goals in five years were, a POE's CEO told us:

Actually, the objectives of the company are not something that you could predict in words, by saying how it should go. It is a gradual process. When the company develops to a certain extent, it would be difficult even if you do not want it to develop further.

In this case, we can see that Chinese companies act by responding to a situation rather than take matters into their own hands. However, this kind of business behavior does not mean that Chinese companies do not have any plans. Most of them do have plans, but they know the plans are just plans. They are subject to change, and the managers are prepared to make these changes. A joke told by a SOE manager illustrates this. The manager had arranged a trip for his business partners to visit his parent company in China. He had made a detailed plan, down to the hours, but when the actual visit occurred, "everything had been changed".

It is worth noting that there are pros and cons to not having detailed business plans. Interpreted positively, it means a high degree of flexibility. It allows the company to both adapt swiftly to the customer's needs on the spot and quickly adjust plans at the right moment. According to a business consultant:

The Chinese are smart. If they felt it was wrong to say something this way this time, they will change to another method next time. If language is not a problem, they can adjust their plans on the spot during their discussions with their customers. For instance, if a Chinese company found that his customer wanted cups during a business meeting, he would say immediately that "we can make cups and we can do it very well." However, in reality, he does not stock any cups at all.

On the contrary, besides pragmatic considerations, what makes the lack of business plans problematic is also the standards of business taken for granted in the Netherlands. As a business consultant put it:

The biggest obstacle Chinese companies faced when they came to the Netherlands is they could not state clearly what they wanted to do here… You cannot say you can do anything, because the others would think you can do nothing. You appear unprofessional.

If being professional is defined as having clear expertise in a specific area and stressing that particular strength by a well-designed system of marketing and branding measures, many Chinese companies do appear unprofessional. Theirs is a way of fumbling ahead, surfing and adjusting themselves to the tides, rather than defining a destination before rushing into the water.

2. Cost of operation

Case study: Business plans

V2Future is a start-up company. Its founder and CEO, Mr. Fan used to be a senior manager at a large Chinese company, also in Netherlands. In 2013 he quit his job and established his own company with several partners. At the beginning, Mr. Fan thought he and his partners could help Chinese companies to develop themselves in Europe. They thought they could provide valuable handles as they all had successful experiences of helping Chinese companies in exploring western markets and they were familiar with both Chinese and Dutch (European) local business cultures. However, after two years of trial and error, he discovered that potential Chinese investors were not willing to pay for such services. In other words, he had a misconception of the market. As he recalled:

We visited 100 to 200 entrepreneurs of all different scales, talking to their CEOs and founders. We told our stories and strategies.... Upon hearing our stories, they all acknowledged that we had value, and showed willingness to let us help them or use our services. However, they didn't want to pay. So, we realized that our business plan had problems.... The companies that are really willing to invest and are able to sustain its development are rare. Most Chinese companies are holding an opportunistic attitude. They just want to give it a try. If they succeed they will continue, if not they will go, so they do not want to invest at the preparation stage. This is what we did not expect at the beginning.... However, we could not earn any income in such a situation.

Having little income, but huge costs, some initial co-founders left the company. However, since 2014, Mr. Fan found another way of generating income and this way proved to be successful in 2015. The company helped famous European brands with their online marketing in China based on Chinese internet platforms like *baidu. com.*

When European companies are willing to pay for Baidu, they will also pay for Tencent and Alibaba. For European companies, all sorts of (business) services have value, but Chinese companies have not reached such a level.

In early 2016, when we interviewed Mr. Fan, his company had redefined its business plans and found two new directions. Firstly, the introduction of Chinese high-tech products to Europe, such as unmanned aerial vehicles and virtual reality products, and secondly assisting European companies to do business in China from Chinese internet platforms, such as Baidu and Tencent. Meanwhile, the company's website is undergoing a complete overhaul in response to the many changes to its staff and business activities since its incorporation four years ago. As this case study shows, many Chinese investors feel reluctant to spend money on market research prior to their arrival in the Netherlands. Saving costs on "intangible" business services is probably a legacy from the poor old days. For some companies which arrived in the Netherlands in the late 1990s, the most vivid memories often revolve around the huge price differences between China and the Netherlands.

3. Lack of experience

Of the general managers we interviewed, most said that uncertainty and perplexity were the dominant experiences they felt when their businesses first started doing business in the Netherlands. In some cases, parent companies had little experience of operating internationally. The following quote is from a general manager whose subsidiary was the second one its parent company had set up in the world and the first one in Europe.

When I just arrived here I was only 27 years old. I didn't know anything then …. At that time few Chinese companies were operating abroad. Our boss was like… he threw us all in the sea: "swim!" If you can swim across the river and reach the other bank you survive. If you drown, you are dead. We had great freedom then. Nobody inside the company had experience, so we had to rely on ourselves, fumbling ahead.

Many Chinese companies reported a lack of experience at the initial stages, but the kind of experience they were lacking varied. A POE manager told a tortuous story about how their parent company found a location for its subsidiary. The parent company in question wanted to invest in the Netherlands and they were contacted by the South Netherlands Investment Agency and invited to locate their business somewhere in Limburg. However, only upon arrival did they realize that the place was close to the Belgium border and "too far away". Therefore, they changed their plan and opted for the Randstad. "We mistook South Holland Investment Agency for the West Holland Investment Agency." However, lacking experience could also lead to unintentionally violating labor regulations. In one case a manager hired student-interns without applying for work permits. However, their accountant did send tax returns for the interns to the tax office. On reflection, the manager remarked:

I didn't know how things work here myself. If I had been aware of it, I would not have needed to use them (the local business services). However, it is also a question of habit. In the past years, we did not pay much attention to regulations in China, but it is the most important thing in the Netherlands. However, we have no solution. We had no ability to pay attention to these issues as we do not know what we do not know. Sometimes, it was just because we tried to do everything clearly according to the law, that we exposed all our faults.

Indeed, almost every Chinese company we interviewed stressed the importance of learning the local laws and regulations and named compliance as the first and foremost key to success. However, due to little knowledge or lack of common sense there are consistent worries about unknowingly violating the rules. When asked if they had asked for advice from other Chinese companies or some Chinese company associations, this manager said "we did and they told me it's all about luck."

(Tianmu Hong, Frank Pieke, Trevor Stam, "Chinese Companies in the Netherlands". *Report-Chinese-companies-in-the-Netherlands-2017-final-. pdf*)

Words & Expressions

forge ahead		向前迈进；锐意进取；奋发进取
ammunition	n.	弹药，军火
expertise	n.	专门知识（或技能等），专长
fumble ahead		摸索前进
misconception	n.	误解，错误想法；错误印象
entrepreneur	n.	企业家
aerial	adj.	航空的；飞机的；空中的
overhaul	n.	（制度或方法的）全面改革；大修；彻底检修
intangible	adj.	无形的；难以确定的
perplexity	n.	困惑；令人费解（或困惑）的事务
tortuous	adj.	费解的；曲折的
in question		正被谈论的，讨论中的；考虑中的

Case 6

Intercultural Communication on Web Sites: A Cross-Cultural Analysis of Web Sites from High-Context Cultures and Low-Context Cultures

Introduction

A popular cultural framework was proposed by Edward Hall (1976, 2000), in which he stated that all cultures can be situated in relation to one another through the styles in which they communicate. In some cultures, such as those of Scandinavians, Germans, and the Swiss, communication occurs predominantly through explicit statements in text and speech, and they are thus categorized as low-context cultures. In other cultures, such as the Japanese and Chinese, messages include other communicative cues such as body language and the use of silence. Essentially, high-context communication involves implying a message through that which is not uttered. This includes the situation, behavior, and paraverbal cues as integral parts of the communicated message.

These differences in communication styles across cultures are expected to pose challenges to the ways in which Web sites communicate their messages most optimally. How do Web sites created for a target group in a high-context culture differ from those created for low-context culture audiences? What strategies do high-context cultures use to compensate for lack of context on Web sites that were created in cultures where the norm is to communicate in a manner that is high in content and low in context?

This article presents a set of preliminary results describing the tendencies by which communication through Web sites is adapted to various cultures. The underlying premise of the article is that when customizing a Web site to appeal to a different culture it is not enough merely to translate the text; the overall communication strategy should be appropriate to the audience as well. The study identifies whether and how variables that characterize high- and low-context cultures are reflected on Web sites. It further attempts to draw parallels between face-to-face communication and communication on the web by looking at communication rules and patterns in high-context cultures and comparing and contrasting them to the communication style of Web sites in low-context cultures.

Cultural Awareness in Web Design

At about the same pace as the popularity of the Internet increased, visions flourished of the World Wide Web as a tool for bringing the world together. The marketing world in particular quickly embraced the Internet as an ideal medium for reaching beyond domestic markets in order to disseminate products to hitherto foreign markets. The localization strategies for this may have been simple at first—first generation Web sites, which were simple and text-based, needed a mere translation to be cross-cultural. However, the development of Flash and the implementation of video and sound have brought new potentials to the Web and set new standards for efficient and effective Web communication.

Nowadays a Web site is not just a collection of text; it is a conglomerate of images, multimedia, interactive features, animated graphics, and sounds. From a marketing-strategic perspective, a company that defines itself as cross-culturally aware knows (or should know) that creating appealing and efficient Web sites for other cultures is no longer just a matter of language and modification of time- and date-formats. Cross-cultural Web design nowadays requires dealing with design issues that include culture-specific color connotations, preferences in layout, animation, sounds, and other effects that are characteristic of today's generation of Web sites.

In order to do this successfully, the designer must study the target group of the Web site. While user participation is ideal in the designing process, a study of the design elements prevalent in the culture may also provide the Web designer with some useful guidelines. Values and behavior indoctrinated through cultural influences may be reflected in design practices.

By understanding how communication styles may be reflected on Web sites, we come a step further towards identifying, and subsequently realizing the potentials of, the interactive nature of the Internet. This would be rewarding not only from the marketing perspective, but also for those organizations that are working on bringing the world closer together through dialogue. Intercultural communication competence, as Chen and Starosta (1998) note, is imperative for human progress, and it is by studying communication styles and understanding how to use them that we may be able to communicate more clearly, and promote dialogue between "us" and "them". The interactive and global nature of the Internet has fostered many visions of mutual understanding among cultures, although the means for achieving this are still at a very early, exploratory stage.

In this article, the findings of anthropologists Edward Hall and Geert Hofstede on cultures provide the basis for the analysis of Web sites. Their findings include a set of categories into which we can systemize cultures—for example, preferred message speed (Hall, 1976) and collectivism/individualism (Hofstede, 1980).

A number of studies on the relationship between Web site design and cultural dimensions have been conducted. Studies similar to the present one include Marcus and Gould (2000) and Sheridan (2001), who analyzed both commercial and non-commercial Web sites in an effort to identify relationships between Hofstede's cultural dimensions and visual presentation on the Web in order to deduce guidelines for Web design. The present study differs from the previously mentioned studies by being one of the first to approach cross-cultural, visual Web design with Edward Hall's theoretical framework, rather than Hofstede's, as its point of departure. Hall's focus on communication in his cultural model is particularly relevant with regard to Web design, as will be shown.

1) *A Note on Cultural Frameworks*

The research conducted by Hall and Hofstede, which led to the formation of their oft-cited cultural dimensions, is frequently criticized for being outdated (the dimensions were proposed in the 1970s and 1980s, respectively), and especially archaic in their practice of utilizing geographical borders between nation-states as boundaries for cultures. By contrast, in the light of the accelerating process of globalization, cultures are increasingly recognized as fluid and amorphous entities (see, e. g. , Morley & Robins, 1995)—never absolute, but constantly in transition.

It is acknowledged here that rigid categorizations of populations foster stereotypes, and also that the world has moved on since the 1970s and 1980s. Thus far, however, there has been no convincing demonstration that relative differences with regard to the prevailing norms in cultures do not exist in practice, and on the basis of this that Hall and Hofstede's cultural parameters should be discarded completely. On the contrary, the qualitative study of local(ized) Web sites around the world presented in this article shows that in spite of these important criticisms, communication patterns today still resonate with the cultural dimensions proposed decades ago.

2) *Characteristics of HC and LC Communication*

Hall observed that "meaning and context are inextricably bound up with each other" (Hall, 2000, p. 36), and suggested that to understand communication one should look at meaning and context together with the code (i. e. , the words themselves). By context, we refer to the situation, background, or environment connected to an event, a situation, or an individual. When communication is HC, it is not only the nonverbal and paraverbal communication that comes into play. HC communication draws on physical aspects as well as the time and situation in which the communication takes place, not to mention the relationship between the interlocutors. The closer the relationship, the more HC the communication tends to be, drawing on the shared knowledge of the communicating parties.

By using scales meant to conceptualize the difference between HC and LC communication, Gudykunst et al. (1996) identified HC communication to be indirect, ambiguous, maintaining of harmony, reserved and understated. In contrast, LC communication was identified as direct, precise, dramatic, open, and based on feelings or true intentions.

3) *Directness vs. Indirectness*

Hall adds that those who use LC communication style are "expected to communicate in ways that are consistent with their feelings", whereas a person from a HC culture will set the context and the setting and let the message evolve without referring to the problem directly. In the event of a conflict arising, HC cultures tend to use indirect, nonconfrontational, and vague language, relying on the listener's or reader's ability to grasp the meaning from the context. LC cultures tend to use a more direct, confrontational, and explicit approach to ensure that the listener receives the message exactly as it was sent.

4) *Thought Patterns and Language*

LC cultures tend to emphasize logic and rationality, based on the belief that there is always an objective truth that can be reached through linear processes of discovery. HC cultures, on the other hand, believe that truth will manifest itself through non-linear discovery processes and without having to employ rationality.

In conversations, people in LC cultures will shift from information already stated to information about to be given, while HC communication will jump back and forth and leave out detail, assuming this to be implicit between the two interlocutors. These patterns of linear versus circular thinking may in some ways reflect the way monochronic cultures perceive the concept of time compared to polychronic cultures—as a linear sequence of progressing happenings from start to deadline, versus the circular or sporadic patterns that are evident in the cycle of the year, month and life. HC cultures are thus characterized by indirect and cyclical approaches in their conversation and writing styles, often communicating without mentioning the subjects directly, whereas LC cultures will get straight to the point.

5) *Collectivism vs. Individualism*

The collectivism vs. individualism dimension was proposed by Geert Hofstede (1980), and suggested as an alternative to the HC/LC dimension. The two dimensions, however, correlate: HC cultures tend to be collectivistic while LC cultures tend to be individualistic.

Collectivistic cultures prioritize group welfare over the goals of the individual.

The family's history often has an influence on the way people see an individual, whereas personal accomplishments will play a minor role. Individuals in collectivistic cultures tend to be interdependent with others and will usually have built a network of deep-rooted relationships and personal, loyal ties. Values in collectivistic cultures include training, physical condition, and the use of skills.

LC cultures, however, tend to be individualistic, where emphasis is put on the goals and accomplishments of the individual rather than the group. Individuals are expected to be independent of others and look after themselves. When accomplishing goals, consideration of others is often limited to include only oneself and one's immediate family. Personal values include personal time, freedom, and challenge.

6) *Power Distance*

Another of Hofstede's dimensions, which is tied to the HC/LC dimension as well as to the collectivism/individualism dimension, is the power distance dimension. This refers to the extent to which less powerful members expect and accept unequal power distribution within a culture (Marcus & Gould, 2000). The characteristics of cultures with high power distance include many hierarchical levels, autocratic leadership, and the expectation of inequality and power differences, and are affiliated with HC cultures, such as Japan. In contrast, low power-distance cultures are characterized by flat organization structures, consultative or participative management style, and the expectation of egalitarianism, especially evident in LC cultures such as the Scandinavian countries.

7) *Polychronic Versus Monochronic Time Perception*

Hall (1976) noticed that the perception of time is culture-specific. He identified cultures belonging to either end of the spectrum as being either polychronic or monochronic, where HC cultures are polychronic and LC cultures are monochronic. Monochronic cultures view time as an important, almost tangible phenomenon; they are generally oriented towards planning and scheduling, so as to promote efficiency, while people in polychronic cultures believe that everything will happen "when it's time".

8) *Message Speed*

A final dimension worth considering, as proposed by Edward Hall and Mildred Reed Hall (1990), is that of the message speed preferred by a given culture, i.e., fast versus slow messages, which are respectively tied to LC and HC cultures. Messages that are quickly and easily decoded and acted on are categorized as fast messages, and include headlines, TV commercials, and prose. Slow messages, which take a little more effort to act on and decode, include books, TV documentaries, and poetry.

A fast message sent to people who are geared to a slow format will usually miss the target. While the content of the wrong-speed message may be understandable, it won't be received by someone accustomed to or expecting a different speed. The problem is that few people are aware that information can be sent at different speeds. (Hall & Hall, 1990, p. 4)

Hall and Hall (1990) note a connection between message speed and relationship building: "In essence, a person is a slow message; it takes time to get to know someone well." (1990, p. 5) Fast message cultures such as the United States are usually adept at creating quick contacts, but may also be perceived as superficial. Slow message cultures such as many European cultures and Arab countries may take their time to build relationships, but this generally results in these being deep-rooted and long lasting.

9) *Hypotheses*

The characteristics of HC and LC cultures outlined above raise questions regarding the contrasts between the characteristics of HC cultures and the Internet, which was developed in LC cultures. Some of these can be formulated into the following hypotheses, and provide a focus for the subsequent analysis in this paper.

Hypothesis 1

Given that HC cultures place strong emphasis on the personal relationship between the communicating parties, we can hypothesize that:

H1: HC cultures will, to a higher degree than LC culture Web sites, implement strategies for assimilating human presence on their Web sites.

HC cultures can be expected to emphasize imagery and other, nontextual forms of communication to provide context in general. We can perhaps also expect that HC cultures draw on the many potentials of the Internet by integrating animation and other communicative effects in their Web sites. These effects—such as multi-media, flash animations, and interactive functions—have the potential to provide a sense of human representation or interaction.

Hypothesis 2

H2: HC cultures are likely to use more imagery and less text than their Low-Context counterparts.

The indirect nature of HC communication, the predominance of preferred slow message speed, and the prominent use of symbolism in HC communication anticipates that images, animations, and other nontextual media will be considered of high importance on HC Web sites. By comparison, Web sites created for the LC market are expected to be richer in text and with fewer occurrences of animations, heavy images, and other effects, to ensure that LC Web sites are kept as practical and direct sources of information.

Hypothesis 3

H3: The imagery chosen on HC culture Web sites will reflect values characteristic of HC cultures, such as family values, whereas LC culture values will be present on LC culture Web sites.

How might the influence of collectivistic or individualistic values be reflected on Web sites in terms of the imagery chosen? In the light of the high correlation between collectivism in HC cultures, and individualism in LC cultures, we might expect a tendency towards representing individuals by themselves in those Web sites belonging to LC cultures, while group pictures of individuals would be more common on Web sites belonging to more HC cultures.

Hypothesis 4

H4: The pages making up LC Web sites are expected to be consistent in their layout and color schemes, whereas pages in HC Web sites are expected to be diverse.

We might expect some similarities between the architecture of a Web site and the thought patterns belonging to a given culture. Logical, linear thinking patterns would imply linear navigation throughout the site, with a consistent layout throughout the pages of the site, thus promoting a structured and timesaving quality. Parallel thinking patterns would imply a complex, less discernible navigation, offering subtler clues as to where the links will guide the visitor. Priority should be given to the aesthetic experience of the Web site in HC cultures, rather than the informative function, which we would expect to be prioritized in LC cultures.

Method

The study was conducted as a cross-cultural, qualitative analysis of Web sites from countries categorized as belonging to either HC or LC cultures. The Web sites analyzed included ones from Japan, China, and Korea as representatives of HC cultures, while Germany, Denmark, Sweden, Norway, Finland, and the United States provided representatives of LC Web sites. The differences between the two

Web site samples were explored and sought to be explained in terms of Hall's dimensions.

The analysis in this project focuses on visual communication, dealing not only with the representation of the product featured on the Web site, but also of the Web site itself—mainly in connection with navigation. Visual communication here refers to the conveying of messages through all visual cues except written text.

Visual communication on Web sites is expressed through layout and the use of images, photographs, and animation. This analysis examines how the uses of these different communication tools differ between HC and LC cultures. The present study is exploratory, and is based on the analytical model of visual communication on Web sites presented by Lisbeth Thorlacius (2002). This model in turn is shaped by Roman Jakobson's verbal communication model, and thus provides a systematic and comprehensive approach for identifying the various communicative functions present on Web sites.

The analysis was carried out by the author between November 28 and December 19, 2003. The inevitable cultural bias of the author in conducting the analysis should of course be kept in mind, especially in a study such as this one, which involves a high level of interpretation.

The cross-cultural analysis of Web sites is restricted to those of McDonald's multinational corporation, whose fast-food restaurants are to be found in 119 countries (http://www.mcdonalds.com/corp/about/mcd_faq.html). (Hermeking, this issue, observes that cultural differences in Web site design are most conspicuous with regard to nondurable products such as fast food.) We can assume that a successful and globe-spanning company such as McDonald's has done extensive focus group testing of their Web sites and consequently customized each Web site to appeal to its user group in each target culture, to ensure that product communication is as efficient as possible. It is on the basis of these assumptions that McDonald's Web sites were chosen as suitable subjects for this study.

The branding of the product featured on a commercial Web site can influence the design of the site as a whole. McDonald's may choose to profile itself by emphasizing its American identity, resulting in choices in the construction of the site that reflect Western values and interface design. For instance, the Pakistani McDonald's Web site (http://www.mcdonalds.com.pk) has chosen an interface design very similar to the Microsoft Windows 2000 desktop metaphor, with icons placed in the upper left hand corner of the screen and a "Start" button at the bottom left hand corner, which unfolds into a menu when clicked. In this way, McDonald's perhaps hopes to brand itself as something new, modern, and Western, appealing to youth and their identity as part of a new, globalized generation.

For this reason, issues such as culture-specific symbolism, colors, and metaphors on the Web sites have not been dealt with in this article, as such studies would require several informants originating from each studied culture. For discussion of issues of this nature, readers are referred to the work of Russo and Boor (1993) and Vanessa Evers (2001).

Results

The following examples illustrate different ways in which cultural influences are reflected in Web design.

1) *Animation*

Animated effects on Web sites tend to be more prominent and elaborate in HC cultures than in LC Web sites, where such options are reserved for relatively subtle effects such as emphasizing active links or drawing attention to logos. Much of the animation on HC Web sites is centered on images of people. For instance, HC Latin American sites such as the Chilean and Brazilian ones use animation in connection with images of young people dancing or jumping. The same tendency can be found on the Chinese site, which displays the moving silhouette of a break-dancer. This form of illustration is not seen in the North American and European countries, and in particular Scandinavia, where the McDonald's sites are completely static, or where animation is minimal and images are of individuals in relaxed situations. This tendency can perhaps be explained by the cultural values prevailing in those nations as proposed in Hypothesis 4, either reflecting the importance which is placed on one's health and physical condition in collectivist societies, or by the cherished nature of personal relaxation time by members of individualist cultures.

As with the rest of the findings in this analysis, there is bound to be a minority of examples that do not comply with the rest. If, for instance, we take the McDonald's site from Hong Kong, which we identify as HC, we are in fact presented with an image of a young person relaxing in a couch with his hat covering his eyes. According to the tendency, this image would be categorized as belonging to an LC culture Web site. This site also reveals that Britain has its influence on Web sites, as well as many other things, in Hong Kong, by providing the visitor with an alternative version of the Chinese site, one entirely in English. We can therefore consider the image of the relaxing person as an expression of British/LC cultural influence.

One interesting use of animation on HC Web sites is the assimilation of non-verbal, behavioral language, which is characteristic of HC face-to-face communication. An Internet function, animation is used to communicate in alternative ways from text, by providing high context using cues that assimilate or derive from real-life conversations.

Although this practice appears to be relatively rare, the Japanese McDonald's Web site illustrates how animation in the form of short videos can provide an alternative to communication through text and still images, to create the impression that the visitor is virtually met by a personal representative of the company. The videos are mainly used as short introductions on each page, but the most interesting ones are the one on the welcome page and the one on the contact information page.

The short video on the welcome page shows four men in white clothes and caps, carrying a massive "M" and placing it on the floor, after which they quickly bow and hurry behind the logo. On the contact information page, we find a well-dressed woman stepping out from behind the logo towards us, and then taking a long bow. The video is then replaced with a large picture of the smiling woman, with her hands in her lap, as if waiting for interaction with the visitor.

A similar approach used by Kurosu and Kashimura on the interface of their cash dispenser (1997) involved an image of a bowing woman to signal that data were being processed. The bowing representatives of the company communicate an acknowledgement of the visitor, a "welcome" and an "at your service" statement.

The vividness of HC Web sites is often completed with the implementation of music and sound effects. Some sites play a limit of a couple of seconds of the "I'm lovin' it" jingle or background beat, and the Korean site has implemented the whole jingle (in Korean) to be played from beginning to end. This trend is supported in Vanessa Evers' research, which shows that 86.5% of Asians (Chinese, Indonesians) strongly liked sound effects, whereas only 64.9% of the Australian control group strongly liked sound effects (Evers, 2001).

Whether animation is used on Web sites is dependent on at least two issues other than the user's belonging to HC or LC cultures: the user's patience, which perhaps can be determined by time-orientation, and the user's technological access and limitations. The designer who decides to implement unsolicited animations and effects must assume that the user sees the necessity of them, and that the user is technologically able to process them to the user's satisfaction.

2) *Promotion of Collectivistic and Individualistic Values*

It is worth considering the values that are portrayed along with the product, and how these connect with those ideologies relevant to the target group culture. Values prevailing in HC cultures are generally tied to collectivism and those in LC cultures to individualism, hence we can assume that HC and LC culture Web sites manifest different values according to their ideologies.

Collectivist cultures tend to emphasize being in good physical shape and time spent with family and friends as their dominant values, whereas the notion of freedom and personal time valued in individualist societies implies relaxation and time spent by oneself. As noted above, images of individuals dancing or doing sports are more prominent on HC Web sites than LC Web sites, whereas in LC countries individuals tend to be portrayed in more relaxed situations or situations connoting holiday activities, such as a trip to the lake or listening to music.

It is particularly interesting to see how McDonald's uses different approaches to profess its slogan "I'm lovin' it." The slogan not only promotes the food, but a whole lifestyle. The Swiss-German site displays images of individuals enjoying themselves with music and relaxation, and offers an in-depth explanation of the philosophy behind the new slogan: "You're immediately at the center of attention—your individuality, your everyday life, situations in which you recognize yourself and where you would like to see yourself."

This definition is absent in sites such as the Indian one, where an image of a man running with a boy in a shopping cart is placed next to the slogan, creating a visual connection between the two texts. Both the man and the boy, with a Happy Meal on his lap, are laughing wholeheartedly as they speed down the supermarket aisle. The slogan seems to reflect the thought of both of the participants, and seems to reflect the fun of being together as a father and a son, uncle and nephew, or some other close relationship.

The Indian site certainly emphasizes a different enjoyable experience from the kind found in the Swiss-German site, which rather praises that time which is spent by oneself, for instance by listening to music with earphones large enough to block out the outside world.

We can further compare and contrast the two sites by examining their emphasis on social issues such as community work. It is interesting to see that despite McDonald's deep involvement with community work, the extent to which this is communicated is different depending on the collectivist or individualist orientation of the user's culture. On the Swiss-German site, a link to the Ronald McDonald fund is placed near the bottom of the page, as the last point on the menu. When clicked, the user is presented with a very short description of the Ronald McDonald fund, and a referral to the official Ronald McDonald Fund Web site.

Adhering to the image change connected with the new slogan, McDonald's India may have replaced a group photograph of happy employees with one of a man and a boy, but in return, the "Community" link has been promoted to a much more prominent location on the home page, placed second on the menu of links. For being a LC culture site, the information on community work can be considered very extensive, spread across four different pages.

Similar findings are shown in the research done by Leonardi (2002), who identified differences between Web sites designed for Hispanic and non-Hispanic Americans. There, the imagery of groups rather than individuals alone was identified as important for successful marketing of mobile phones to Hispanics.

3) *Images of Individuals Separate or Together with the Product*

If we examine the three images representing a man relaxing on the roof of a car, what distinguishes the pictures from the German site and Swiss site from the picture on the Chinese site is that the latter example includes the presence of a McDonalds product, which is missing in the German site and Swiss site.

We might have expected the opposite to be true—that those sites created for LC cultures would be more inclined to make a direct connection between the individual and the product, whereas on HC Web sites the designer would rely on the user to grasp the connection between the two elements. We can perhaps explain this effect by referring to Marcus and Gould, who suggested that individualism and collectivism may influence the importance given to individuals versus products shown by themselves or in groups (Marcus & Gould, 2000). As we have seen, collectivistic societies place high importance on people and relations, whereas individualistic societies tend to value products and consumerism. When displaying a product together with an individual, it reflects the values of HC cultures by drawing focus away from what the product offers and towards what the person receives when enjoying the product.

The portrayal of individuals together with products is not, however, exclusively present in HC culture Web sites, just as images of individuals or products by themselves are not exclusively present in LC culture Web sites. Those HC culture sites that are especially heavy on illustrations will almost inevitably include a variety of both kinds of pictures. Rather, we can describe the trend as highly probable in HC sites, and expect that at least one image of an individual together with the product will be found on the homepage or main pages of an HC culture site. On LC sites the same would be described as an exception, where such images are saved for career pages or restaurant pages.

4) *Transparency*

Transparency refers to the extent to which the users are required to make an extra effort in order to find the information they are looking for. The McDonald's Web site from Denmark, a LC culture, can be described as a very transparent site, as it provides a detailed overview of the rest of the site on the home page. The home page features a large collection of links, and describes clearly what lies behind them through the use of headings, subheadings, and illustrations. This makes it possible for the visitor to find what he or she is interested in immediately.

Most HC sites, in contrast, depend on links and information described by a limited amount of text, and sometimes with an illustration. This gives a less transparent overview of the content in the Web site compared to LC sites, and often requires that the user "chase" the information through exploration of the site and performing mouse-overs (placing the cursor over a link to reveal more content information before finally clicking it).

This tendency coincides neatly with the idea that, in LC cultures, it is the sender who does all the work in clarifying information and getting the point across, while in HC cultures, it is the receiver who has to work to retrieve the information. This finding also coincides with Hypothesis 2 proposed earlier in this article, in which it was hypothesized that images would substitute for words on HC Web sites to a large extent.

An example of a site that relies on the exploration of the user is the Japanese McDonald's site. Here, a menu filling half of the interface serves to direct the user to news releases and new features. As a starting point, this menu consists of nine squares in different shades of gray, one of which is larger than the rest and featuring an image of the latest addition to the McDonald's Restaurant menu. When resting the cursor on one of the other squares, the image disappears, while the square touched by the cursor grows into a new image. When the cursor is moved away, the entire menu morphs back to a set of gray squares. The observer will notice that the graphic and its link, seen in the top left-hand square out of the nine, changes every five seconds or so between two new menu items and a promotion for World Children's Day. The menu therefore relies on the patience of the user and willingness to explore the site to find what he or she is looking for.

Although menus like the ones described above illustrate how the Internet can provide the visitor with HC communication, they cannot be considered representative for HC Web sites. In most instances, menus like the examples above are supported by other, more LC versions. It seems that HC cultures might have grown accustomed to the way in which Web sites are designed in Western societies and adopted many of the same functional menu structures before exploring how communication on the Web can be reconfigured to conform to HC communication patterns. For this hypothesis to be confirmed or negated, however, would require longitudinal research on the development of HC Web site designs.

5) *Linear versus Parallel Navigation Around the Site*

The differences in thought patterns between HC and LC cultures, as outlined in the beginning of this article, are clearly reflected in the design of Web sites. Whereas the Scandinavian sites are tabular and functional in their design, the Asian sites rather seem to take a montage/layer-upon-layer approach in their layout, using many bright colors, fonts, and shapes.

The layer-upon-layer look is best perceived when looking at the sites in action. The designers behind the Asian sites seem keener on illustrations and links that constantly morph into new ones, where parts of information are hidden underneath other information on the same page. Their Scandinavian counterparts tile information side by side on one page, so that nothing covers anything else as a starting point. The Asian sites are also inclined to use pop-up windows, which are practically non-existent in the Scandinavian sites—compare the site from Taiwan, China, where virtually all links open up in new browser windows, and the Norwegian site, which consistently opens pages in the same window. This is consistent with similar contrasts documented by Bucher (2002) in his comparisons between German and Chinese Web sites.

Implications for Web Design

We are now able to draw parallels between the cultural variables identified at the outset of the article and the findings outlined above. Since many of the cultural dimensions and characteristics are strongly correlated, each variable may induce more than one tendency, and the tendencies may imply the influence of more than one variable.

Nonverbal communication such as body language may represent itself on HC Web sites through imagery and animated effects on the Web site.

Thought patterns are especially reflected in the navigation of the site, for instance through the subtle or obscure guidance and opening of new pages in new browser windows common on HC Web sites. Navigation reflecting the linear thought patterns that prevail in LC cultures is evident in the restricted number of new browser windows as well as apparent and specific navigational guidance.

The collectivism/individualism variable is reflected in the values that are reflected in the imagery of the Web site, such as images of individuals versus images of groups, products placed together with individuals, the situations in which the individuals are placed, and the extent to which emphasis is placed on community work.

The power distance dimension is apparent in the hierarchical structure of the Web site. High power distance is reflected in tall hierarchical Web site structures, either through the implementation of many pages with unstructured layout, or the opening of new browser windows for new pages, instead of in the same browser window. Low power distance is reflected in flat or shallow hierarchical structures, either through the implementation of few pages with coherent layout or the opening of pages within the same browser window.

The time perception variable, which is tightly bound with thought patterns, is apparent in the navigation of the site. It is also apparent in the transparency of the site, and whether the designer relies on the user's patience and willingness to explore the site to seek information.

The message speed dimension is apparent in the transparency/nontransparency of the site, implying the amount of effort expected from the visitor to understand navigational clues. The inclusion of a virtual, personal representative of the company, as illustrated on the Japanese McDonald's Web site, can perhaps also be considered a reflection of slow message speed in relation to the emphasis on relationships.

Discussion

The evidence presented here indicates that Web sites in HC cultures differ from Web sites in LC cultures in a variety of ways, five of which are outlined in this

第四章 高语境文化与低语境文化——交际方式与思维方式之别

article, and probably many more of which are yet to be discovered. It is evident that differences in communication styles between HC and LC cultures do occur on the Web. Moreover, the current study suggests that the multimedia character of the Internet is helpful in terms of communicating online in a HC manner.

(Elizabeth Würtz, "Intercultural Communication on Web Sites: A Cross-Cultural Analysis of Web Sites from High-Context Cultures and Low-Context Cultures". *Journal of Computer-Mediated Communication*. Volume 11, Issue 1, 1 November 2005. Pages 274 – 299. Https://doi.org/10.1111/j.1083-6101.2006.tb00313.x. Published:)

Words & Expressions

paraverbal	*adj.*	接近言语的；与言语相关的
optimally	*adv.*	最优地，最佳地，最适宜地
premise	*n.*	（作为先决条件的）假定，假设
customize	*vt.*	按顾客的具体要求制造（或建造、改造等）
disseminate	*vt.*	散布；传播；撒播（种子等）
hitherto	*adv.*	迄今，到目前为止
conglomerate	*n.*	混合体；聚集物
animated graphics		动画图形；动态图像
indoctrinate	*vt.*	向……灌输；教导
imperative	*adj.*	必要的；紧急的；极重要的
deduce	*vt.*	演绎，推论，推断
archaic	*adj.*	过时的，陈旧的
in the light of		鉴于；由于；根据
fluid	*adj.*	易变的；不固定的，不稳定
amorphous	*adj.*	难以归类的；不规则的；无固定形状的
parameter	*n.*	范围；参数；变量
qualitative	*adj.*	定性的；质的；质量的
inextricably	*adv.*	分不开地；无法摆脱地
interlocutor	*n.*	对话者；参与谈话者
conceptualize	*vt.*	使概念化
ambiguous	*adj.*	含糊不清的；不明确的；模棱两可的
nonconfrontational	*adj.*	非对抗的
rationality	*n.*	合理性
linear	*adj.*	线的；直线的

implicit	adj.	不明言的；含蓄的
monochronic culture		单维时间文化
polychronic culture		多维时间文化
circular	adj.	迂回的；不直截了当的；循环的
sporadic	adj.	不时发生的，偶发的；零星的；散发的
autocratic	adj.	独裁的，专制的；专横的
affiliate	vt.	使紧密联系；使隶属（或附属）于
egalitarianism	n.	平等主义；平均主义
spectrum	n.	范围；幅度；系列
decode	vt.	解读
gear	vt.	使准备好；使适应，使适合
adept	adj.	熟练的，擅长的，内行的
hypothesis	n.	假设；前提；猜测
assimilate	vt.	使相似；使同化
counterpart	n.	对应的人（或物）
predominance	n.	主导地位；（数量上的）优势
discernible	adj.	看得清的；辨别得出的
globe-spanning	adj.	横跨全球的
brand	vt.	加商标于
interface	n.	界面
informant	n.	信息提供者；资料提供人；合作者
silhouette	n.	剪影；轮廓
assimilation	n.	吸收；同化
dispenser	n.	自动发放器；分发者
jingle	n.	叮当声
unsolicited	adj.	未经请求的，没有被要求的；主动提供的
connote	vt.	包含；意味着
profess	vt.	承认；表示；显示出
referral	n.	提及；参照，参考；印证
cursor	n.	光标；指针
neatly	adv.	巧妙地；熟练地
retrieve	vt.	检索；找回；使恢复
morph	vt.	转变成，改变
reconfigure	vt.	（计）重新设置，重新配置

tabular	*adj.*	列成表格的；表格式的；扁平的
montage	*n.*	合成画面；画面剪辑；蒙太奇手法，剪辑组合物
font	*n.*	字体；（同样大小和式样的）一副铅字
in action		在运转中；在积极活动中
tile	*vt.*	（计）平铺
outset	*n.*	开始，起始；开端

第五章　时空观念的中西文化差异

跨文化交际中，时间与空间观念是非语言交际的重要维度。不同文化对于时间与空间的观念与感知是不同的，人们的行为会有意无意地受到其所属文化关于时间和空间观念的制约和支配。中西文化差异也体现在人们的时间观念和对私人空间的界定与划分方面。了解不同国家和民族在时间和空间观念上的差异，在一定程度上有助于减少跨文化交际中的失误，从而提高跨文化交际能力。

一、时间观念

美国人类学家霍尔（Edward T. Hall）将时间分为两大范畴——单维时间观（monochronic time）和多维时间观（polychronic time），用以说明来自不同文化背景的人们，他们的时间观和对待时间的态度是不同的。美国、英国、加拿大、德国等西方国家属于单维时间观国家，中国等亚洲国家，以及拉丁美洲、非洲和南欧国家属于多维时间观国家。

单维时间观认为，一方面，时间是有限的，可以量化，而人的需求是动态的，不断变化的，因此，人的需求可以调整，以适应时间安排的需要，所以就有了诸如计划、安排、期限等事宜。而另一方面，时间又是线性的，可以切割划分，但是时间如河水一样流淌，一去不复返。因此，西方人的时间观念很强，强调时间效率，强调有效利用和管理时间。他们往往将时间分段，在每一个时间段安排不同的活动，按计划和时间安排行事，一般在一个时间段内做一件事，做完一件事再做另一件，而且，每完成一件事需要取得一个结果。单维时间观的国家大多倾向于现在时间取向（present orientation view）和未来时间取向（future orientation view），考虑问题主要着眼于当前和未来，而不是过去。这样的时间观和价值取向也常常体现在企业的对外传播中，正如 AT&T 的愿景所述：

We envision a world where everything and everyone work together. We envision a world that works for you.

多维时间观认为时间就是工具，可以根据人的需要进行调整或改变，不必先完成一件事再开启另一件事，可以根据实际情况的需要或许可，同时做几件事，正所谓"耳听六路，眼观八方"。处于多维时间观文化中的人们，他们的时间概念比较笼统和模糊，处理时间有许多不确定性，对他们来说，时间具有很高的可塑性，可以因人因事做出调整，所以，他们做事计划性不强，灵活多变，常常"计划赶不上变化"。多维时间观的国家大多倾向于过去时间取向（past orientation view），重视历史文化传统。中国是一个典型的多维时间观国家，中国文化重视吸收历史的经验教训，尊崇先祖，讲究资历。这种时间观也体现在中国的对外传播中，中国企业和机构的对外宣传大多从"发展历程"或"历史沿革"开始，例如："1912年2月，经孙中山先生批准，中国银行正式成立。从1912年至1949年，中国银行先后行使中央银行、国际汇兑银行和国际贸易专业银行职能……"

二、空间观念

有关空间的概念及其界定与个人空间和隐私密切相关，同时，人们通过人际空间或距离控制或调整人们之间的相互关系和相处模式。以集体主义为导向的中国人强调群体意识和群体隐私，因此，各团体或机构常常以院墙围合一个群体空间；而以个人主义为导向的西方人则崇尚自我意识和个体隐私，房前屋后要以花园栅栏界定私人空间。

葛兰素史克中国（内地）/香港区人力资源部负责人王毅女士对中西文化在时空观念方面的差异做出如下解读：

"西方人的尊重体现在给人时间和空间，给人选择的机会并尊重别人的选择——不过问别人的隐私，不关心他人的私生活，不主动给人忠告。具体到人与人在工作上的关系，尊重可以体现在开会守时（开始和结束一样守时），有要求提前告知，下班极少电话谈工作等。而中国人的尊重更多体现在表面，有仪式性。如果我们有一个最需要改的坏习惯，那就是缺乏计划性、不遵守时间。试想在西方社会，如果我们对他人的时间都不尊重，我们何谈尊重他人？我们又如何赢得他人的尊重呢？"

有外国人在"知乎"上直呼："吃饭的时候，我怎样才能礼貌地拒绝中国人用筷子把食物夹进我的碗里，他们为什么要这么做？"这个问题直接点出了中外饮食文化的差异，中餐礼仪和西餐礼仪截然不同。西餐一般不分享食物，体现出西方人一贯的独立生活作风，而吃中餐给客人夹菜是中国人表示热情和尊重的一种方式。对此，外国网友除了担心卫生外，也非常在意吃饭的碗即绝对的私人空间被侵犯。然而，也有中国网友"反击"："我们也不喜欢见面就拥抱，你们别抱我，行不行？"

中西文化的时空观念差异在职场上的表现也很突出。在中国，个人的工作与生活空间联系密切，相互穿插渗透，界限不清。例如，职场人几乎需要24小时待机（on call），随时接收与回应领导、同事、客户的信息，个人生活常常需要调整以适应工作的节奏，家庭生活也要为工作需要让位。而在西方，个人的工作与生活空间有严格的界定与区分，互不干扰，人们工作是为了创造更好的生活。

Case 1

The Spatio-Temporal Differences of Chinese Enterprises' Experience in the Netherlands

[提示]

Case 1 提及的文化冲突主要表现在：

1. 中西方的时间与空间观念差异很大，由此产生的冲突不断。例如，海外雇员会严格遵守合同规定的工作时间（"Local employees would not be willing to work a split second longer than their contracts require."）。而在中国，在老板下班之前离开岗位会被视为失礼与不敬（"It is considered impolite in China or even disrespectful to leave the office before your boss."）。

2. 中西方的工作节奏也不尽相同，由此给工作带来诸多不便。例如，圣诞节和新年是西方最重要的节庆，这个长假正好与中国企业最重要、最繁忙的年终结算、出年报时间冲突。

3. 中国企业的缺乏计划性和灵活多变 vs 西方企业的详尽计划（"Planning skills, making best-scenario plans and alternative plans, are extremely valuable in the European market. In comparison, in China, everything is too flexible and changing too fast, so that planning cannot show its value."）。

Temporalities

Chinese companies often experienced culture shock revolving around different conceptions of time, pace and rhythm. Because of the Dutch habit of planning schedules well ahead of time, the most frequently encountered problem for Chinese managers is making appointments, as illustrated by one of our interviews below.

Schedule and planning are really difficult for the Chinese. Between Chinese people, if we are in a good relationship we can call each other and make the appointment immediately. However, the foreigners (the Dutch) think "you need to make an appointment in advance. Otherwise please do not talk to me". At the very beginning I really could not understand. I am your customer, do you really want to do business with me or not? All these showed different ideas and customs in China and the West. However, when we have lived and worked abroad for a while, we discovered that all these are just natural.

Another common problem is the separation between work and life. In many cases, the life of Chinese managers is not ordered by a standardized working schedule. They have to arrange their life around their work and tend to continue working after office hours. However, seeing that their local employees would not be willing to work a split second longer than their contracts require, the managers sometimes become desperate. For one thing, the parent companies may still expect that the speed of work of the subsidiaries complies to Chinese norms. How could that be possible without the cooperation of local employees? For another, it is considered impolite in China or even disrespectful to leave the office before your boss. Although knowing that they could not expect this subtle cultural conformity from their Dutch local employees, it proved difficult for the Chinese managers to switch off their emotions.

Even more serious confrontations revolve around the rhythm of life and business throughout the year. A case in point is the time for end-year financial report. Christmas and New Year's Eve are the most important holidays of the year in the Netherlands, while in China this is exactly the moment when most companies are crazily busy finalizing their annual financial reports. The most significant holiday in China is the Spring Festival, which is about two months after the Christmas. An SOE's CFO:

As a listed company, working overtime during Christmas and New Year is so normal (for us), because we need to publish our external report. However, it is so difficult to ask our Dutch employees to do this in the Netherlands. It is not as if we would like to pay extra for the overtime that they would be willing to work. They want to put their families first. We could also understand that. But there are conflicts in this respect.

The manager told me that they try to solve the problem by sharing the financial statistics with the head office, removing part of the functions that should be the responsibility of Dutch employees to China. As a result, the Dutch division does the routine work, while the Chinese head office deals with more intensive work and deadlines. However, the expat Chinese managers are not always very content with such a solution.

When we share some financial statistics, we can only read the numbers. But what are the things behind the numbers? We still need local employees to explain them.

Moreover, different concepts of temporalities bring different paces. A Chinese subsidiary wanted to move office within an office building for rent in Rijswijk. According to him, eighty percent of the building was empty due to the declining economy at the time. However, they had to wait for more than a month simply to get an initial price offer.

Desperate about "Dutch speed", the manager remarked:

This building's employees should not have much to do. They only have a few renters. How could such things happen?! ... I think the Netherlands lack stimulating measures. It's the same regardless of whether you work more or work less. It is a serious problem. Even our own salesmen do not respond to incentives.

Many Chinese companies participate in all sorts of business events to build networks. They try to visit potential business partners and are constantly adjusting their plans either upon the requests of the customers or based on their sharp observations during meetings. The parent companies mostly evaluate the subsidiaries by their financial results and give them all the freedom to explore different measures in order to achieve the goal. However, the path towards "localization" as aspired by almost every Chinese investor proves to be long and cumbersome.

Improvement of Organizational Skills

Improvement of organizational skills mainly means bringing local Dutch managers with international experience on board. With their help, companies start designing and executing external development strategies as well as internal operating rules. This is often remarked upon as a new stage of a company's development in the Netherlands. For most Chinese managers, good management means planning and control, which are regarded as the hallmark of modernity. As mentioned, Chinese companies come to the Netherlands often without systematic planning. In fact, they are not so much proud of their own flexible ways as they are admiring the assumed Dutch measures of thorough planning.

A POE manager attributed the employment of a Dutch manager who had worked for Sony as a critical moment in his company's development and cited an obviously well-known joke among Chinese managers. The joke is about the European version of life in heaven verses life in hell.

The European version of life in heaven is a British policeman, an Italian girlfriend, German cars, French food and Dutch management.

And the European version of life in hell is when you have a German policeman, a British girlfriend, Italian management, French cars and Dutch food.... The Netherlands is very famous for its management.

The Dutch level of management also tops the whole of Europe.

What the manager refers to as good management is actually all about developing long term plans. According to him, the European market is different from the Chinese market in reaction speed.

In the Chinese market, you adopt some adjustment this week and the next week you can see some effects. However, in the European market, you implement an adjustment today, and you have to wait for half a year to see some impact.

That is why planning skills, making best-scenario plans and alternative plans, are extremely valuable in the European market, he explained. The same manager believes that in the Netherlands a whole team of employees can work as a precise instrument with good plans and management. In comparison, in China, everything is too flexible and changing too fast, so that planning cannot show its value. As an expression goes, "The plans cannot catch up with the changes."

(Tianmu Hong, Frank Pieke and Trevor Stam, "Chinese Companies in the Netherlands". *LeidenAsiaCentre Press. Report-Chinese-companies-in-the-Netherlands-2017-final-.pdf*)

Words & Expressions

temporality	n.	时间观；时间性；暂时性
a split second		一瞬间，一刹那
conformity	n.	符合；一致；遵守；依照；
incentive	n.	奖励，鼓励；刺激

| cumbersome | adj. | 麻烦的；累赘的 |
| hallmark | n. | 特点，特征，标志 |

Case 2

Time Orientation Toward Task or Relationship

[提示]

Case 2 体现了两种时间观的冲突：保证效率与效果的时间观和维护关系与和谐的时间观之间的冲突；联系过去与未来的循环的时间观 vs 立足现在走向未来的时间观之间的冲突。

The dimension of time speaks to how communities are oriented toward space and time, including their tendencies toward traditions and the past, and their orientation toward the future and the present. In many cultural systems, holding on to traditions is important in current day-to-day operations and relationships. Some societies will refer to traditions to preserve and maintain cultural norms, that is, to protect what currently exists.

Time is also a reference to a culture's orientation toward tasks or relationships. For example, a manager from the United States who travels to India to negotiate a business contract needs to know that meetings will occur whenever people show up to the meeting, which could be hours after it is scheduled. A task-oriented leader is certain to be frustrated when he meets up with an Indian who is more time-oriented toward relationships. In the American perspective, promptness is professionalism; yet, in the other perspective, the concept of time is more loose and flexible.

Time is an important value dimension of culture and, as a result, impacts the behaviors of people. time is regarded in some cultures as punctuality, while, in others, time is more relaxed and is viewed as contributing to the building of relationships. The following case studies illustrate the notion of time and the behaviors of cultures based on their interpretations of time.

Tim, a white man, manages a production department in an American private business. Many of his assembly line workers come from the Southeast Asian and Asian cultures. Whenever his employees had a problem, they would want to talk and discuss the project at length. They not only wanted to understand the problem but they wanted to keep harmony in the organization. They would come back to him several times even after the problem was resolved. For this manager, the problem had a quick solution: he provides the solution and his employees should comply. However, he doesn't understand why his employees keep coming back to him about the issues. He's annoyed at the amount of time it is taking to manage the process.

Tim and his employees have been raised with different notions of time. Tim thinks that time is associated with efficiency and effectiveness. To him, when an issue is discussed and a solution is provided, he believes there should be no further discussion. For his employees, the act of coming back to the problem is not to find more solutions; rather, it is to continue to develop a relationship with the manager—it is to ensure that the relationship is harmonious and in balance. For them, it is a check-in point in the relationship.

LeBaron (2003: 7 – 9) noted that cultural understanding of time can impact conflict management and negotiation processes. As an example, she described a negotiation process between First Nations people and the local Canadian government. She wrote:

First Nations people met with representatives from local, regional, and national governments to introduce themselves and begin their work. During this first meeting, First Nations people took time to tell the stories of their people and their relationships to the land over the past seven generations. They spoke of the spirit of the land, the kinds of things their people have traditionally done on the land and their sacred connection to it. They spoke in circular ways, weaving themes, feelings, ideas, and experiences together as they remembered seven generations into the past and projected seven generations forward.

When it was the government representatives' chance to speak, they projected flow charts showing internal processes for decision-making and spoke in present-focused ways about their intentions for entering the negotiation process. The flow charts were linear and spare in their lack of narrative, arising from the bureaucratic culture from which the government representatives came. Two different conceptions of time: in one, time stretches, loops forward and back, past and future are both present in this time. In the other, time begins with the present moment and extends into the horizon in which the matters at hand will be decided.

(From "Leading with Cultural Intelligence". *Saylor Academy*, 2012. https://

*saylordotorg. github. io/text_leading-with-cultural-intelligence/s*04 2015-3-20）

Words & Expressions

First Nations　　　　　　　　　　　第一民族；原住民

Case 3

Punctuality, Another Way of Acknowledging Rank

Punctuality is another way of acknowledging rank. Punctuality is generally more important in what Edward T. Hall (1959) calls monochronic cultures, which are those in which people generally do one thing at a time, and less so in polychronic cultures in which people deal with several tasks at once. The underlying causes are again rule-based and relationship-based mechanisms.

People in rule-based cultures seek security and predictability by structuring their environment, and in particular by structuring their time. They tend to set aside a time slot for each activity, resulting in appointments and strict schedules. This kind of structuring can succeed only if people are reasonably punctual. Punctuality is not required as a stress-management tool in relationship-based cultures, but it can nevertheless mark rank. Subordinates may show up on time to make sure the boss is not kept waiting, while the boss may show up late to make sure there is no loss of face by having to wait, or simply to display superior status. Supervisors in Indonesia, for example, may habitually arrive half an hour late to meetings, with the ritual excuse of being held up in traffic. One should be cautioned, however, that punctuality may be expected of everyone in some relationship-based countries, such as China and particularly Japan.

(John Hooker, "Cultural Differences in Business Communication", December 2008. Https://public. tepper. cmu. edu/jnh/businessCommunication. pdf)

第六章　中西商务谈判风格的差异

谈判是两个相关方面对面(双方要么有共同利益,要么有冲突),一起在自愿的情况下,在约定的时间和地点,通过恰当的交流方式,通过一定的说服技巧,就特定交易达成共识,最后能满足各自需求的互动和博弈的过程(贾文山,2019)。

中西文化差异也直接体现在商务谈判之中,深入了解相关国家的文化和商业习惯有助于达成互利互惠的商业合作。西方文化强调竞争,美国文化更是如此。他们虽然也相信双赢,但还是想要赢得更多,而且常常把对方的收获视为自己的损失,有时,这种极强的竞争意识与双赢理念并不相符。而中国文化强调建立联系,从长计议,随机应变,灵活机动。

一、谈判目标的差异

中国人的谈判目标是建立和发展一种长期的合作关系,谈判的过程就是相互试探、相互了解、建立互信和人际关系的过程,合同是随着关系的发展而制定的,签订合同意味着长期合作的开始。而对西方人来说,谈判的目标就是签订合同,完成一笔交易,签订一个合同就是解决一个问题,完成一个项目或任务。如果不能签订合同,实现近期的经济目标,建立长期关系就没有意义。西方人大多以结果为导向。

二、谈判策略的差异

在谈判策略上,中国人首先会注重营造友好互信的谈判氛围,互表诚意与好感,并就合同双方需要共同遵守的总体原则和共同利益展开讨论,为建立长期合作打下良好基础,而将具体问题安排到以后的谈判中去解决,即"先谈原则,后谈细节",这是高语境文化的具体体现。此外,高语境社会中的契约具有不同的特征或含义。其一,没有必要把所有条款或细节都写下来,相互理解就足够了。合同更像是一份谅解备忘录而不是具有约束力的法律文件,双方有可能依赖预先存在的信任关系,而不是法律条款来解决问题。其二,由于条款不够详尽清晰,随着形势的发展还有调整的空间,世界在不断变化,为什么要把自己束缚在一纸合同上呢？中国人的谈判观念也很灵活，可以边谈边判断，而这种谈判方式让西方人对中国人的谈判目标很疑惑：不谈具体细节，问题怎么会得到解决呢？

而西方人则恰恰相反，他们将商务谈判视为合同双方交流沟通的场景与机会，并且一开始就迅速切入谈判主题，就合同条款各个细节，由局部到整体，一个一个地落实，体现了低语境文化的特征。他们认为正是因为合同条款包含了各方面的标准和要求，明确了彼此的权力与义务，合同才有约束力，才能带来商业利益。这种线性思维和"直接""简明"的表达方式会让东方人觉得西方人只是想做一笔交易，而这并不是长期合作，因而不可信赖。

Case 1

International Negotiation: How Do I Get Ready?

[提示]

1. 跨文化商务谈判面临的最大挑战是什么？有些美国人不了解谈判对手的文化传统，自以为双方在谈判策略上达成了默契，结果却让他们抓狂：签完合同，韩国人还在不断提出新的要求；美国人自以为做出了最后的让步，却让俄国人和中国人看到了迫使对方做出进一步让步的希望，而这并不是美国人所期待的与之相应的回报。

2. 文化差异会影响谈判的走向和结果，主要表现在五个方面：明确谈判目标，建立良好人际关系，确定谁是谈判的决策人，掌握一些谈判的技巧，以及判断结束谈判的时机。

Example: An International Negotiation Failure

A marketing manager for a large U. S. technology company was visiting one of Germany's biggest corporations. He wanted to sell them on using his new product in their system. Since product and application were quite new, no market pricing was established yet, so the vendor was hoping to get a premium for their technological leadership.

The presentation went well, and the decision maker on the German side seemed interested. He asked for the price. "We think that this product will be well received. We'll be able to sell it to you at 12 dollars," the American responded. For a long moment, the German remained silent. "Well, if pushed hard, we will actually be able to go as low as 10 dollars with this product."The German still didn't say a word.

Twenty-five painful seconds later, the American couldn't take it any longer: "Long-term, we are confident that we will be able to push the price down to 7 dollars." The German now looked puzzled but pleased.

This is not a fictitious story—it happened a few years ago. The American company eventually won the business, but at a price around 2 to 3 dollars lower than what would have been achievable. Volumes being sizeable, the negative profit impact amounted to more than $1 million! The funny thing was that the marketing manager, proficient in his field but lacking international experience, probably thought he got tricked into lowering his price by a smart negotiator, while the German may still be wondering how he got such a great deal without ever asking for it.

If your goal is to grow your international business, no situation presents greater risks to strategy execution and bottom line than a cross-cultural negotiation. Two factors often amplify this:

The negotiation partner is largely an unknown quantity; their strategies and objectives are unclear.

Interacting with the other culture is a first for one or both of the parties involved, and they are not well-prepared for it.

The challenge to understand the other party also exists in domestic negotiations. However, understanding strategies and objectives across cultures is much more difficult. Ignoring the need for culture-specific preparation is a deadly sin in any international business negotiation. There are many skilled and resourceful negotiators in the United States. Alas, without prior cross-cultural experience or preparation, most of them tend to assume that both sides share an implicit agreement over what represents legitimate negotiation tactics and that both sides believe in, or at least respect, the value of a win-win approach. Furthermore, they likely trust their ability to correctly interpret clues about where the other side stands in the decision making process.

None of these may actually be the case in international negotiations. Consequently, an American negotiator may cry foul when a South Korean, for example, continues to make demands after a contract has already been signed. Russian or Chinese negotiators may regard concessions by their American counterparts as a sign of weakness, happily take them without reciprocating, and be even more motivated than before to extort further "free" concessions. Arabs might give small clues that they are willing to close the deal which their American negotiation partners may miss completely, continuing to make new offers. All of these are "normal" misunderstandings across cultures which can wreak havoc with negotiation strategies and goals.

Cultural Differences That Affect Negotiations

Several aspects require careful study when preparing for an international negotiation. Five major aspects deserve closer scrutiny:

(1) *Negotiation Objectives*

In the United States, negotiation objectives are often obvious as the interactions follow a logical, factual approach. Obtaining lower-cost goods or services, gaining access to technology or intellectual property, extending one's influence on markets through alliances, and so on, all share a common denominator: the underlying objective is near-to-mid-term business success as defined by the business' bottom line. Profit and growth are the ultimate motivators, and people are usually flexible and creative in finding ways to meet their objectives. Negotiators are prepared to "slice and dice" the package of terms and conditions being negotiated, willing to make concessions if these help advance the negotiation as long as the overall value of the package still meets their objectives. Long-term aspects of a business relationship matter but play a secondary role. American businesspeople may not engage in an agreement if it holds long-term promise but does not offer an advantage in the near term.

Foreign negotiations can look quite different in contrast. For starters, long-term aspects of the engagement commonly weigh more heavily. Also, negotiators may have a less holistic view of the package being discussed. Let's say an Asian buyer is interested in buying equipment from an American company that requires extensive training and maintenance provisions. The initial negotiation may focus exclusively on the price of the equipment, in spite of efforts on the American side to use tradeoffs in training or maintenance cost to offset pricing concerns. The set of objectives on the Asian side may indeed include a specific price target, and they may not be willing to move on to negotiating other aspects before that target has been met. This sometimes becomes an issue of "face", where not reaching their goal affects the self-esteem and reputation of the negotiators. Such a situation can become uncomfortably emotional for the American side.

Other factors may work to the advantage of a U. S. negotiator without them even realizing it. For example, entering a joint venture or other collaborative agreement with an American corporation can be quite prestigious for business leaders in certain countries. They will usually be smart enough not to reveal that aspect, but with careful preparation and with the help of others, you can identify this upfront and use it to your advantage.

Overall, it is important not to assume that the objectives of the foreign side will be identical with those you would expect in a domestic negotiation. Spending the time and effort to learn about them prior to engaging will give you a strong advantage.

(2) *The Importance of Relationships*

While some form of a working relationship is required for negotiations in the U.S., it does not have to be extensive and can usually be established quickly. In most cases, evidence that you are a valid business partner and an indication that you are willing to negotiate in good faith suffice.

Successful negotiations abroad usually require a lot of up-front relationship building, which is why Americans often complain that international deal-making can be painfully slow. In most of the cultures in Asia, Europe, and Latin America, strong relationships are not only important to ensure proper execution of an agreement but are a prerequisite for entering into any formal or informal negotiations. To varying degrees, people will want to learn about your company background and capabilities, prior experiences, strategies and objectives, long-term plans, and so on. They also want to get to know you personally before they decide to trust you. In several cultures, people don't want to conduct business with you unless you convinced them that you are seeking a long-term engagement rather than just "pursuing a deal".

Several preparation steps are important. You'll want to formulate your long-term plan for the engagement, even if that means covering a longer time frame that your normal business process might call for. Everyone understands that things change, so as long as you're willing to maintain a minimum level of consistency, don't fear that you'll find yourself "locked in". (Be prepared for people to track changes closely, though, especially in Japan.) Next, prepare extensive background information about yourself and your company. Especially in many Asian countries, people expect to get such information in the initial introductions.

If your interactions extend over a long time period, avoid changing team members. This applies not only to the primary negotiator, but to everyone interacting with the other party. Any changes in contacts mean that relationship-building may have to start over, slowing the progress.

Furthermore, realize that the definition of what constitutes a good relationship varies widely between cultures. In certain European countries such as the Nordics, the Netherlands, Germany, also in Israel, frank and direct exchanges indicate trust and a positive relationship, which is opposite to cultures such as China, where politeness and diplomacy are virtues and where there is little trust in "objective" truths anyway. A puzzling fact in China may be that confidentiality is not a requirement of a trusting relationship, as many American companies have painfully experienced. Information is considered free and using it in one's best interest (which includes sharing it with other parties) is considered legitimate. Confidentiality agreements may not change that but will be read as signs of mistrust, hampering the relationship.

Lastly, it is important to know that the relative status of both sides can be different in a foreign culture. In the U.S., the seller-buyer relationship is usually one of near-equality. Successful transactions follow the principle of "win-win", with both sides gaining something (e.g., a good or service) and giving something (e.g., money). In Japan and South Korea, to a lesser degree also in other Asian countries, the seller is hierarchically inferior to the buyer. Such a distribution of roles can make for an irritating experience to the foreigner. In Japan, a salesman is obliged to serve all of the buyer's needs and provide whichever information they request. The buyer, on the other hand, has a cultural responsibility to ensure that the seller still makes a profit from the business, but otherwise can manage the interaction with the seller in a way that may strike some Americans as almost dictatorial. Foreign companies not willing to accept this distribution of roles may get nowhere in their attempts to win business in Japan.

(3) *Decision Makers*

A frequent source of frustration for Americans negotiating in certain Asian and Latin American countries is that they find it hard to get access to the decision maker, feeling that they are talking to the wrong person or group. Back home, identifying the key decision maker is usually easy and getting hold of access to them can always be arranged as long as you have something of value to offer to them.

Accordingly, inexperienced negotiators in international situations may suspect that for some reason the "right person" simply doesn't want to talk to them, thinking they are stuck with an intermediary with limited authority. The reality may be quite different: a "decision maker" in the American sense, i.e., a person with the authority and willingness to make a direct decision, may not exist at all. Decisions are made by groups in many cultures. "The person at the top" still exists—organizations in these countries often have powerful leaders and clear hierarchies. However, the role of that person is not so much to make decisions themselves, but rather to orchestrate and manage the process of how group decisions are being made and implemented. Since group decisions require a series of interactions between all stakeholders to form opinions and establish consensus, they cannot be made right at the negotiation table. Sufficient time needs to be given between negotiation rounds for the group to go through iterations of the process and reach their conclusions. Gaining insight into this process is difficult, so it is pivotal to identify relevant members of the group making the decision in order to try to influence each of them in your favor.

In Europe and Latin America, only managers at the top or at least high up in the organization may have sufficient authority to make decisions. Except for matters of companywide importance, they might not be available for the negotiation itself, relying on inputs from their middle management instead. That still gives you a chance to (indirectly) influence their decision.

(4) *Negotiation Techniques*

People around the world are very creative when it comes to negotiating, bargaining, and haggling. Americans may be at a slight disadvantage in this field, since people in many other countries receive extensive negotiation training already as children, watching their parents bargain at the market or in a shop. Numerous negotiation techniques are used that would be considered unusual or exotic in America. Here are but a few examples.

a. *Deception, False Demands, and False Concessions*

While these may occasionally be encountered in the United States as well, people in certain foreign cultures tend to use them more forcefully. Pretending they are not at all interested in your business proposition is a way for an experienced negotiator to gain an advantage. A false demand, meaning that the other negotiator discovered something you want that they don't value highly, serves as a strong pressure point for you to make a major concession. False concessions, such as repeatedly lowering the (inflated) price without getting any reciprocal concession from you, may lead to feelings of guilt and stimulate you to give up something of value without receiving equivalent value in return. In all of these situations, it is important to recognize the technique. Once you do, you can either call the bluff (caution—this may disturb the relationship) or carefully outmaneuver your counterpart.

b. Extreme Openings

Starting a negotiation with an extreme demand is common practice in some Asian and Arab countries. There are two ways to counter the technique, the efficiency of which depends on the specific culture: either counter-bid at the extreme other end of the spectrum (if they ask a ridiculously high price, offer a ridiculously low one and smile), or state firmly that if they indeed believe the value of their product or service to be that high, then there is no common ground for any further discussion. Inevitably, you will be asked what you consider a more realistic.

Note that in some cultures, people will be irritated and may even be offended by extreme openings. An example is Sweden, where people expect you to start with a close-to-final offer.

c. Aggression and Strong Emotions

In the U. S. , negotiations commonly follow a logical and factual flow. Emotions are being read as an indication of the process going astray. In many foreign countries, the use of aggression and strong emotions may be viewed a legitimate tactic. It is therefore wise not to let oneself be alarmed. If you continue to stay friendly and focused, the other side will quickly drop the tactic as ineffective.

d. Silence

The example in the introduction of this paper is interesting to analyze. In American "cultural language", silence signals a negative response. Extended silence makes the message stronger. In Germany and in numerous other countries, silence does not carry much of a meaning. In the particular situation, the German manager may have been reflecting upon the price or thinking about something completely unrelated. Keep in mind that if the conversation takes place in English and if English is a foreign language for the other side, translation also takes time and may occupy the minds.

Foreign negotiators who previously gained negotiation experience with Americans may attempt to use silence against you. It is best to not read anything into breaks, even extended ones, in the conversation flow.

e. Best-Offer Pressure

"This is my best offer", stated in a negotiation in the U. S. , usually means "take it or leave it". When negotiating abroad, it may not mean that. Negotiators in some Asian countries are known to sometimes make a series of "best" offers, each being a little better than the previous one. Be careful when using the phrase yourself—rather than understanding that this is your final word, the other side may mistake it for a tactic.

f. Time Pressure

Don't share your flight arrangements with your host when negotiating overseas. The Japanese and Chinese are particularly good at this: pretending to help you "reconfirm your travels", what they really want to know is how much time you have budgeted for the negotiation. If, say, you are on a Wednesday morning return flight, they may spend most of the time on Monday and Tuesday making introductions, presenting the history of their company, discussing insignificant details of your proposal, and so on. You may not get to negotiate central parts of the agreement before late-afternoon on Tuesday, by which time you will be more likely to make concessions under time pressure. Most cultures prefer a more relaxed approach to the often-hurried U.S. style, making it easy for them to use your preference for quick and effective interactions against you. It is best always to let the other side know that you have plenty of time and will be able to change flight bookings if needed, even if that may not really be the case.

(5) **Reaching Closure**

When approaching the final stages of an international negotiation, you'll need to carefully look for clues that the other side is ready to close. Too many variants exist to be discussed here, but just like in a negotiation back home, you will pay a price if you miss such signals. Realize that in several cultures, "yes" won't mean "I agree", but rather only signals "I hear what you're saying". It does not convey consent.

How closure itself works again varies greatly. The good old handshake, still in use in America but normally accompanied by signing a contract, works well to confirm agreements in countries such as Brazil, most Arab countries, India, and many others. That does not mean that no written agreement should be prepared, but it is advisable to consider the handshake, rather than the signature, the critical step, while the paperwork becomes a mere formality. The other side might be alienated if you focus too much on the written contract, feeling that you don't trust their word. In Japan, a signed written agreement is not important. Once both sides clearly stated and spelled out their agreement orally and then put it in the meeting protocol, you can be assured that they will follow it to the letter. Generally, you should not bring a legal counsel to any international negotiations. Exceptions exist in a few countries if you hire a local one, but you are almost always better off by consulting legal specialists outside of the core negotiation exchange.

A final caveat is that closing an agreement and signing a contract may still not end the negotiation. In China and especially in South Korea, a contract is viewed a "snapshot in time". New demands may still be brought up later, so keep some maneuvering room.

Conclusions

Proper preparation for your international negotiation requires studying in-depth material about the target culture and/or engaging a coach who commands extensive knowledge of the country and its business practices. The five aspects described in this paper deserve particular attention, but there is much more that you need to know, such as customs and manners in the other culture, levels of formality, how to present information, and so on.

(By Lothar Katz. Http://www.leadershipcrossroads.com/arti_nbp.asp)

Words & Expressions

vendor	n.	销售商；供应商；摊贩
premium	n.	溢价；额外费用；附加费；保险费
fictitious	adj.	虚构的；虚假的
execution	n.	执行；实施；完成
amplify	vt.	放大；增强
legitimate	adj.	正当合理的；合情合理的；合法的
concession	n.	让步；妥协；承认
reciprocate	vt.	回报；回应
extort	vt.	敲诈；勒索；强夺
wreak	vt.	造成（巨大的破坏或伤害）
havoc	n.	灾害；祸患；浩劫
scrutiny	n.	仔细观察，详细审查
denominator	n.	分母；共同特性
near-to-mid-term	adj.	接近中期的
slice and dice		切片和切块，切割
prestigious	adj.	有声望的；有威望的；声誉高的
suffice	vt.	足够；足以
prerequisite	n.	先决条件；前提；必备条件

hamper	vt.	妨碍；阻止；阻碍
dictatorial	adj.	独裁的；专政的
orchestrate	vt.	编排；策划；精心安排
stakeholder	n.	利益相关者；股东
iteration	n.	反复；重复
haggle	n.	讨价还价；争论；（尤指）讲价
outmaneuver	v.	以谋略制胜；智胜
counter-bid	v.	还价，反报价
spectrum	n.	范围；光谱；声谱；波谱；频谱
astray	adj.	迷路的；离开正道的
variant	n.	变种；变体；变形；变量
alienate	vt.	使疏远；使不友好；离间
caveat	n.	警告；告诫
snapshot	n.	快照抓拍
maneuver	vi./vt.	巧妙地移动；操纵；使花招

Case 2

Global Contract Practices

[提示]

在不同国家和地区，商业合同的作用和重要性截然不同，人们对合同的理解和期待也不尽相同。

Agreements must be kept. People around the world agree on this legal principle, which goes back all the way to the Roman Empire. Unfortunately, while everybody may agree in principle, interpretations of the meaning of "agreement" vary greatly across countries and cultures. At the individual level, this easily leads to misunderstandings and mutual disappointment. In the business world, different expectations and interpretations may also have severe consequences.

Role and Importance of Contracts in Different Countries

More so than anywhere else, contracts in the United States serve multiple purposes. They confirm the exact nature and scope of the agreement, document resulting rights and obligations, often including provisions for many eventualities, and serve as the primary enforcement tool. Accordingly, Americans consider business contracts important and prefer them to be highly detailed. The country's legal system recognizes contracts as the valid representation of the agreement between the parties involved. Breaches of contract can quickly trigger threats of legal action, which is deemed acceptable once other attempts to resolve the issues have failed. The fact that one company is suing another does not necessarily mean that they will cease to do business with each other. The importance that Americans attribute to them is in stark contrast with how Japanese businesspeople view contracts. In Japan, contracts primarily document the underlying agreement and resulting actions. Given the Japanese inclination to avoid uncertainty, contracts tend to be very detailed. They don't need to be signed, though. While the country's legal system dependably supports the enforcement of contracts, Japanese companies almost never sue each other. Instead, they rely on the strength of mutual business relationships to resolve disagreements. If they cannot resolve issues, the Japanese look for mutually respected arbitrators to achieve out-of-court resolution.

Chinese practices are similar to those in Japan. Contracts serve for clarification purposes. They do not exist to enforce the underlying agreements. While all relevant information should be included, Chinese contracts are usually not as detailed as those in Japan or in the U.S. The Chinese legal system has made significant progress in the last 10 to 15 years and the legal enforcement of contracts now seems possible, at least technically. Nevertheless, Chinese expectations remain unchanged: since contractual terms & conditions aren't "etched in stone", business partners should work together to resolve differences and remain flexible as required to accommodate changes affecting the execution of the agreement.

The realities of the business climate and legal system in Russia let the enforcement of contracts through legal action seem a lofty proposition. Most Russian businesspeople pay limited attention to contracts, keeping them high-level and documenting only the essentials of the underlying agreement. Should disagreements arise, pointing to a contract rarely changes behaviors. Instead, the parties may initially try to resolve their issues in a collaborative fashion. If that fails, they might resort to building political or economic pressure on the other side as a way to enforce the agreement.

Implications for Global Companies

Different attitudes towards the role and importance of contracts raise the question of how global companies should deal with others' expectations: how best to get a foreign business partner to keep an agreement? How to make a foreign business partner feel that agreements are being kept?

No single strategy is universally successful. Those insisting that foreign partners must abide by the same standards as domestic ones are rarely effective. Several American companies had to find that taking a Chinese partner to court burned many bridges, not only with that partner and with local or national government representatives, but also with other industry players, making it much harder to do business in the country. In Russia, some foreign companies paid dearly for trying to enforce contractual rights in court when local judges sided with Russian contract partners and issued highly unfavorable rulings.

Successful global companies recognize local realities and adjust their strategies accordingly. They strive to understand their partners' expectations, emphasize business relationships, and remain flexible when disagreements arise. After all, when it comes to closing and executing contracts in foreign countries, it is helpful to remember the old adage:

When in Rome, do as the Romans do.

(By Lothar Katz. Http://www.leadershipcrossroads.com/arti_nbp.asp)

NewWords & Expressions

eventuality	n.	可能发生的事情，可能出现的结果
resolve	vt.	决定；决心；解决
arbitrator	n.	仲裁人；公断人
etched in stone		金科玉律
abide	vt.	遵守
adage	n.	谚语；格言

Case 3

Individual Decision Making vs Group Decision Making

[提示]

谁才是谈判最终的决策者？

When negotiating a contract renewal with a Fortune 20 giant, I spent more than three months exchanging emails, preliminary agreements, and draft Statements of Work with corporate contacts in three different U. S. States, as well as one in Puerto Rico, one in Panama, and one in France. While the subject of the agreement had not changed, some modified terms and conditions required alignment. What had seemed easy proved to be hard. After countless exchanges, a number of points still remained controversial and the bargaining got stuck. We were running in circles. Finally, my key contact at the company suggested setting up a call with another U. S. — American, apparently her boss, whose name had never even come up before. The boss and I talked. Our call took a total of 12 minutes and resolved all open points. The contract was signed a few days later.

As it turned out, the key contact's boss was the real decision maker in this interaction, so he and I were able to quickly reach agreement. For some reason or other, the others involved in the negotiation just had not wanted me to know about this up to that point.

A common experience? Probably not. But it refreshed an important lesson: when negotiating with U. S. companies, do what it takes to identify the decision maker and deal with that personis. Otherwise, you may be spinning your wheels. This may not be true for every U. S. firm, but it certainly is for most of them. In this individualistic business culture, decision making is normally not a team sport, so if dealing with people who don't "have the say", they become little more than messengers complicating the exchange.

Is this a universal finding? Sure not. Business cultures have a strong influence on how people and companies around the world make decisions, as a result of which styles are very different.

(Over-)simplistic cultural models describe two camps: individualistic cultures, which imply lone decisions, and collectivist ones, where decisions are apparently the result of some kind of pow-wow involving everyone. Both assumptions would be naive. The reality of business decision making around the globe is complex and demands careful consideration. Two factors matter most: how individualistic a national (and corporate) culture is, and to what extent decision making is delegated down from the top.

Individual Decision Making

Business decisions in most individualistic cultures are normally made by individuals. In Australia and the U. S. , to some degree also in Canada, Northern Europe, and Israel, authority is also frequently delegated to low levels in the hierarchy. The decider might consider inputs from others, but doing so is usually not a requirement for decision making here. Unlike in my above personal story, identifying the person is normally easy.

In most other individualistic cultures, which pretty much leave most European ones, authority is not as readily delegated. The lead negotiator usually has at least some decision power but often needs higher management approval before sealing a deal. Others may be involved in the negotiation if particular knowledge or competencies are required. This is most pronounced in the U. K. , where decisions often appear to be made committee style, even though there is usually still one person who ultimately makes the decision. In France, managers often informally consult with peers, too, before closing the deal.

While the influence of others should never be underestimated, the common denominator for this group of countries is that reaching agreement ultimately requires winning the support of a single key person.

Group Decision Making

Negotiations in countries whose cultures reflect greater group orientation, which includes almost all of Asia, Latin America, and Africa, as well as parts of Southern and Eastern Europe, for example Greece and Turkey, tend to be more complex than the above. Interestingly, most companies in these countries have strict corporate hierarchies. It would nevertheless be a mistake to consider the people at the top of these organizations to be sole decision makers.

Even seemingly autocratic executives, who are almost the norm in countries such as India, Indonesia, Mexico, or South Korea, solicit and consider inputs from those affected by a decision before making it. In other cultures, for example in China and Japan, decision making is often a process of formal and informal deliberations designed to reach a group decision that has everyone's support. This does not at all mean that every voice carries equal weight—but it will likely be considered. The role of the executive is to orchestrate the process and to make sure the decision is made and communicated.

Business negotiations with members of any of these cultures are regularly conducted in teams, although one-on-one negotiating can be found, too. In either case, there will be others not participating in the interactions who nevertheless influence the eventual decision. Successful negotiation strategies for dealing with these cultures therefore require winning the support of all influential members of the group, as well as that of the person at the top.

As you can see, the biggest difference between individual and group decision making is that with the latter approach, focusing your efforts on only one person is not a promising strategy, no matter how powerful the person is. That may be another lesson worth memorizing.

(By Lothar Katz. Http://www.leadershipcrossroads.com/arti_nbp.asp)

Words & Expressions

preliminary	*adj.*	预备性的；初步的
alignment	*n.*	校正，调整
spin your wheels		浪费时间；原地打转
pow-wow	*n.*	议事会；聚会；商谈
competency	*n.*	能力；胜任
deliberation	*n.*	细想；考虑；商议

第七章 提高信息传播的有效性，讲好中国故事

全球化、信息化时代，各种媒介、各类信息纷至沓来，读者不得不在各种媒介、各类信息之间不断进行选择，以便在最短时间内，最大限度地获取所需信息，这对外宣翻译是一个极大的挑战。外宣翻译是一种国际传播，其实质是信息传播与文化交流，但是这种信息传播和文化交流不是单向的"一厢情愿"，需要考虑和尊重双方彼此的思维和欣赏习惯。要实现文本功能，提高信息传播的有效性，译文首先要能激起读者的阅读意愿，符合读者的认知能力，满足读者的信息需求，适应读者的思维和阅读习惯，抵达读者的情感意境。

实践证明，人与人、群体或机构之间的跨文化交流与合作远比国家和政府之间的交往更为现实有效。实现中国企业与中国文化"走出去"战略的一个重要途径就是要通过讲好自己的故事，讲好本专业、本行业的故事，从而讲好中国故事，传播中国声音，展示真实、立体、全面的中国。

我国传统的外宣翻译注重准确传递文本所包含的各种信息，注重语言转换技巧，但是对译文是否易于为目标读者理解与接受，文本目标是否实现考虑不够，似乎语言转换完成了，信息就自然传递了。译者对译文的文本功能和目标缺乏整体把握，因而，译文的信息传播效果是未知的，也不为译者所重视。

在欧美国家，为了应对社会多元化的信息需求、阅读习惯和信息传播方式，多种写作技术应运而生，如创造性写作（creative writing）、技术写作（technical writing）或职业写作（professional writing）等。这些写作技术通过加强写作的目的性和针对性，提高文本的被接受程度，提高信息传递的有效性。

外宣翻译即国际传播，是一个跨文化交际的过程，其目的是使译文读者能够准确无误、方便快捷地理解和获取译文所传递的信息。在此过程中，译者不仅要设法化解两种语言在表达方式、逻辑关系、语体风格和文化背景等方面的差异引起的理解困难，而且要实现译文的文本功能，适应目标读者的阅读和表达习惯，从而取得最佳的信息传递效果。

一、掌握汉英语言表达习惯和文化方面的差异，提高信息传递的有效性

不同的文化背景和语言表达习惯，形成了汉英各自不同的写作风格和审美

标准，而且对于同一类主题的文本，信息需求和审美习惯也存在着很大差异。为了实现信息传递的目的，外宣翻译需要使用在国际语境中被广泛理解、接受的方式、习惯与话语来阐释与叙事。同时，译者要译出语言和风格都地道的语篇，需要积累大量的英语平行文本，研究英语作者在类似的场景中频繁使用的句型和词语，并进行模仿。

（一）将中文惯用的宏大厚重的叙事转化为英文以具体事实为依据的叙事

基于不同的文化背景，汉英民族的思维与表达习惯各异。具体而言，汉语语篇通常从空泛宏观的信息入手，由远及近，结尾点题，归纳总结；而英语语篇往往以主题句起始，以事实为依据，依层次论证，主题句有明显的标志性。以英译《寻找唐家湾》为例。

【例1】

唐家湾闻名于世是在近代，堪称中国近代名人故里。在那个风雷激荡的年代里，受到风土人情、家风、个人气质、遗传因素的作用，她竟涌现出了那么多人才：实业家、革命家、政治家、教育家、艺术家。从"洋务运动"时期开始，涌现了著名实业家唐廷枢、中华民国第一任内阁总理唐绍仪、清华学校第一任校长唐国安、中国早期工人运动领导人苏兆征、粤剧编剧大家唐涤生、著名版画家古元……不仅彰显个体风采，而且具有集群发起的现象，<u>在纵深一百五十年的历史舞台上演出了一曲多声部的合唱。</u>

Tangjiawan emerged as the hometown of distinguished celebrities in modern China. Influenced by such elements as local environment, family tradition, personalities and heritages of the time, many talented people have established themselves as industrialists, revolutionaries, politicians, educators and artists. Starting from the Westernization Movement, <u>these distinguished celebrities have made their stunning and dynamic presence on this historical stage for a period of 150 years.</u> They are the famous industrialist Tang Tingshu, the first Prime Minister of the Republic of China Tang Shaoyi, the first president of Tsing Hua College Tang Guo'an, the leader of the early China's Labor Movement Su Zhaozheng, the great playwright of Cantonese opera Tang Disheng, and the famous print artist Gu Yuan, to mention a few.

让我们暂且从唐家湾"中国近代名人故里"这部大书中管窥一段一八七三年前后近代社会的缩影。

第七章 提高信息传播的有效性,讲好中国故事

<u>The scene in Tangjiawan, "hometown of distinguished celebrities in modern China", represents a microcosm of modern society around 1873.</u>

一八七二年,经过多年的买办生涯,精明干练的唐廷枢,已经拥有了上海的丝业、茶业同业公所,还是多家洋行的股东,深孚众望,正游刃有余地步入经商的绝妙通道。他是一个懂得挑选适合自己的东西组成产业和自己生活的人,非常实际,经营嗅觉极为敏锐,功名和经营两不耽搁,这种人注定要度过丰富多彩的一生。从这一年起,其人生发生重要转折,受到李鸿章力邀,他成为洋务官僚的得力助手。在未来的岁月中,连续创下了中国近代产业历史上的几个第一:作为国营轮船招商总局总办,最早经营了工业革命时代的产品蒸汽机轮船;由轮船保险而起,念念不忘发展自己的经营行业,又创办了首家中国人自办的保险公司;主持经营了中国近代煤矿中成效最显著的开平煤矿;为便于矿产运输,修筑了中国自营的第一条铁路线……

In 1872, Tang Tingshu, a shrewd and successful businessman, has been running silk and tea guilds in Shanghai, holding shares in foreign firms, after years of working as comprador. He was a gifted and practical man with a keen business sense, who knew how to make choice and turn it into business, which brought him fame, successful career and a colorful life.

From then on, his life was dramatically changed. On the recommendation of Li Hongzhang (politician, general, diplomat of the late Qing Dynasty, leader of the Westernization Movement), Tang was appointed to assist bureaucrats of the Westernization Movement. For years to come, he successively set up several records in China's modern industry history. As the head of the state-owned China Merchants Steamship Navigation Company (CMSNC), he was the first to manage the steamship, a product of the Industrial Revolution; he established the first Chinese-run insurance company for the sake of having insurance for his ships; he took charge of the operation of the most successful coal mine in modern China, Kaiping Mines; he built the first railway line in China to facilitate the transport of minerals…

一八七三年,当唐廷枢已步入不惑之年时,一群垂髫少儿悄悄登上历史舞台。也许是机缘巧合,他们在唐廷枢曾经作为总办的轮船招商总局门口留下了即将远行的身形。派遣幼童到美国留学,固属"中华创始之举,抑亦古来未有之事",这两句话是曾国藩和李鸿章在给朝廷的奏折里说的。尽管由洋务派送走的留美幼童,对专制统治集团具有很强的依附性,但留美幼童计划客观上是近代文化思想领域新学与旧学、西学与中学、学校与科举博弈的重要事件。它是中国现代教育的发轫,开启了中国学生海外留学的先河,是西学东渐的重

要步骤。直到今天，历史帷幕才撩起一角，让我们看清了唐家人幼儿远渡重洋、破冰之旅的成长履迹。由于香山县濒临澳门，接近外洋，得风气之先，与外界接触较中原而言非常频密，加之买办家族光宗耀祖的垂范作用，更在于中国第一个留美学生香山南屏人容闳竭力推动，当时，唐家人将留学美国视为"洋翰林"的光明仕途，很乐意将子弟送出国门谋求未来的发展出路……

When Tang just turned 40, the year 1873 witnessed a historic event—dozens of officially selected children took a photo right at the gate of CMSNC, once headed by Tang, before making their journey to study in the United States. Sending children to study in the United States is "a great undertaking", as Zeng Guofan (a Chinese statesman, general, and Confucian scholar of the late Qing Dynasty) and Li Hongzhang wrote in a memorial to the emperor. Although this effort, initiated by those who advocated the Westernization Movement, was attached to feudal autocracy, the endeavor of having children exposed to western education was a significant event of modern time, in the field of culture and ideology involving new learning vs old learning, western learning vs Chinese learning, school education vs imperial examination. The event marks the beginning of modern education in China, and Chinese students studying abroad, which is an important step towards the process of introduction of Western learning in China.

Today, reviewing the history gives a glimpse of how children in Tangjiawan made their first attempt to study abroad and develop themselves. Close to Macao and influenced by exotic culture, Xiangshan County contacted with the outside world more frequently than the inland regions. Inspired by successful stories of comprador families and the strenuous efforts of Rong Hong, a native of Xiangshan and the first Chinese student to study in the United States, people in Tangjiawan regarded studying in the United States as a bright career and were willing to send their sons abroad to pursue future development…

【分析】

（1）如果按照中文的思路，将"在纵深一百五十年的历史舞台上演出了一曲多声部的合唱。"译成"These talents have jointly produced a great symphony on this historical stage for 150 years."，英语读者将不知所云。

同样，将"让我们暂且从唐家湾'中国近代名人故里'这部大书中管窥一段一八七三年前后近代社会的缩影。"直接译成"Let's look at the microcosm of modern society around 1873 from the perspective of Tangjiawan—the hometown of modern Chinese celebrities. "，就会与后面段落在意义上无法连接，不便于为后面历数历史人物的丰功伟绩做铺垫。

（2）中文的段落构成是围绕某个主题展开的较为完整的陈述，而英文的段落是按照叙事的层次划分的，中文的一个段落译成英文可能会分几个段落层次论述。因此，将"从这一年起，其人生发生重要转折"（From then on, his life was dramatically changed）和"直到今天，历史帷幕才撩起一角，让我们看清了唐家人幼儿远渡重洋、破冰之旅的成长履迹。"（Today, reviewing the history gives a glimpse of how children in Tangjiawan made their first attempt to study abroad and develop themselves）作为主题句，另起一段，分别陈述事实和历史成因。

（二）将中文语句间的意义连接转化为英文语句间的逻辑关系

中文往往从空泛遥远的时间空间开始叙事，语句之间通过意义连接，而英文则依靠逻辑关系连接。因此，汉译英需要将中文看似不相关联的流水句转化成逻辑关系清晰、结构严谨的句式结构，便于目的语读者理解掌握。

【例2】
<u>千山外，故园中</u>，唐家湾位于特区珠海市的北部。
Tangjiawan, <u>a tranquil town in nostalgia</u>, is located in the northern part of Zhuhai Special Economic Zone.

这片土地的历史可以追溯到五千年前。淇澳岛位于唐家湾的北部，就是在这个水中孤岛的东面，一九八四年在一次文物普查中发现了后沙湾新石器时代遗址，它成为广东省境内甚有代表性的历史较早的史前遗址之一。考古证明了一种或多种史前文化的存在，而史前文化在长达三千年的演绎中展现出多姿多彩的侧面。<u>从千年遗迹到百年聚落，从遥远的推测到鲜润的传统生活，从古迹保护到历史建筑的再利用，让我们穿越时空，直抵唐家湾</u>。

The history of Tangjiawan can date back to 5,000 years ago. Archaeology has proved the existence of some prehistoric cultures, which have evolved for three thousand years, presenting a colorful scene. In 1984, the Houshawan Neolithic site, to the north of Tangjiawan and east of Qi'ao Island, was discovered in a cultural relic survey and became one of the representative prehistoric sites in Guangdong Province. <u>Hence, developing smart solutions to protecting and renovating the historic buildings and town is a process of exploring the millennial relics, centennial settlements, and</u>

traditional life style to get the essence of Tangjiawan.

【分析】

(1) 在第一段的翻译中,"千山外,故园中"看似与"唐家湾位于特区珠海市的北部"没有直接的关联性,仔细品味却能感受到原作深厚的历史情怀和怀旧情感,因此通过一个同位语 a tranquil town in nostalgia 予以体现,以此建立起前半句与后半句在语义方面的关联。

(2) 如果按照中文的叙事方式翻译第二段,将"这片土地的历史可以追溯到五千年前。淇澳岛位于唐家湾的北部,就是在这个水中孤岛的东面,一九八四年在一次文物普查中发现了后沙湾新石器时代遗址"译成:

The history of Tangjiawan can date back to 5,000 years ago. Qi'ao Island is situated to the north of Tangjiawan. In 1984, just to the east of Qi'ao Island, the Housha Bay Neolithic site was discovered in a cultural relic survey.

第一句是主题句,旨在介绍唐家湾的历史渊源,第三句后半句用考古发现加以证实,但是第二句一开始就提及另一个地名——淇澳岛,读者会不明白这是在介绍唐家湾,还是淇澳岛,二者之间有何联系。实际上,淇澳岛是唐家湾的一部分,考古发现就位于唐家湾北部,淇澳岛东面。因此,需要将这里的考古发现前置:Archaeology has proved the existence of some prehistoric cultures,然后标示具体位置:the Houshawan Neolithic site, to the north of Tangjiawan and east of Qi'ao Island, was discovered...

(3) 如果按照中文的表达方式,将"从千年遗迹到百年聚落,从遥远的推测到鲜润的传统生活,从古迹保护到历史建筑的再利用,让我们穿越时空,直抵唐家湾。"译成:"Now let's look at/explore the origin of Tangjiawan from the millennial relics to centennial villages, speculation of prehistory to fresh traditional life, preservation of historical sites to reuse of historic buildings."目的语读者怎能领会本书的主旨是探讨唐家湾古镇的历史文化遗产保护与活化的可行性呢?

(三) 将中文宏大华丽的语言表达转化为英文朴素简约的语言

中英文在行文与遣词方面存在巨大差异。中文文本一般语言表达宏大华丽,善用厚重的形容词和副词,运用多种修辞手法营造意境,给读者带来身临其境的感受,从而达到吸引读者的目的。此外,中文表达主观色彩浓厚,擅长抒发情感。英文表达则讲究逻辑理性,文本大多风格简约,表达直观通俗,用词准确,注重事实性信息和语言表达的吸引力。因此,汉译英需要将中文常见的华丽形象的描述转化为英文朴素简约的表达,删减过多的比喻和修饰,压缩主观性的想象,避免"死译""硬译"。

【例3】
基于唐家湾的地理特征、人文精神及建筑聚落的多元性，<u>一个广阔的天地展现在世人面前</u>；当近代社会初露曙光之时，唐家湾不再犹豫，迅速抓住机会，<u>飞快地越出地平线，喷薄而出</u>。尽管这个海隅一方的村镇从十九世纪后半叶开始，名字之响亮足以和澳门、香港媲美，但对它的价值认识却刚刚开始。

With the special geographical features and humanistic spirit as well as the diversity of historical building clusters, <u>a new image of Tangjiawan emerged</u>. <u>As the modern era approaching</u>, Tangjiawan did not hesitate to seize the opportunity of development. Although this seaside town was prosperous enough to be comparable to Macao and Hong Kong since the second half of the 19th century, its value is just to be recognized.

【例4】
中国很多古村镇多有显赫的历史，但到近代，受地理位置、社会制度变化的影响，多渐趋式微，<u>甚至悬殊之大，上下有若天渊</u>。而唐家湾这样海隅一方的古镇，它的历史不算最长，但却一直能<u>呈波浪型，蜿蜒向前</u>。特别在晚清之后绝大部分乡村地区一蹶不振的特殊情况下，唐家湾没有出现衰退，反而形成中山模范县这一发展高峰，又强化了它的历史痕迹。

Many ancient villages and towns in China boasted glorious past, but faded or dramatically languished in modern times, affected by geographical location and changes of social system. As a century-old seaside town, Tangjiawan developed continually, going through the ups and downs. Especially after the late Qing Dynasty, when most rural areas mired into a depression, Tangjiawan did not decline, instead it developed into a model county—Zhongshan County, a climax of its development, reinforcing its prominence in the history.

二、将技术写作的原则运用于外宣翻译，加强国际传播的针对性，讲好中国故事

（一）技术写作

根据美国密西根州立大学技术写作专业的定义（Profile of Technical Writing at Michigan State University），技术写作是专业化的高级写作，包括数字媒体环境下的写作、以学科或文化内容为依托的写作、以编辑和出版为目的的写作

等。技术写作的核心是信息传播,内容包括所有应用文本、科技文本以及网页文案等,例如:备忘录、建议书、项目策划、可行性报告、各种广告与招商宣传、产品与企业宣传、技术手册和科技文献等。

技术写作与传统写作的不同之处在于:技术写作针对特定读者群,具有明确的目的性;技术写作是用清晰准确的表达、易为读者接受的方式传递信息,确保读者能够快速准确地掌握和使用所传递的信息。

技术写作的原则包括:

(1)理解不同的信息传播环境会产生不同的写作任务,传播环境包括传播方式、文本格式、文本类型、目标读者、写作目的等因素。

(2)针对不同读者群的专业写作,即写作要针对特定文化/职业背景和特定机构组织的读者,注重信息传递效果。

(3)创造性地写作,不同文本,风格各异,清晰准确,易于理解掌握,论证充分,说服力强。

(4)运用文字与图像将纷繁复杂的信息内容转换成易于理解掌握的信息文本。

由此可见,技术写作具有很强的针对性和适应性,而且,其适应性是多方位的,要求文本与信息传播方式相适应,与读者的文化背景和认知能力相适应,与读者的信息需求相适应,提高文本的可读性。这些目标设定是为了提高信息传递的有效性,因此,技术写作对以传递信息为主要目标的外宣翻译具有实际的借鉴作用。

(二) 实例分析

讲好中国故事,传播中国声音,翻译是一个重要环节。完整、准确、深入地向世界说明中国,实现中国文化与世界文化的汇通与融合,是外宣翻译的责任。最好的国际传播不是按照中文原文一一对应地进行语言转换,而是在充分理解原文意旨的基础上,对原文进行适当加工,包括对原文内容与文字的增删和重组,甚至重写,按照国外受众的思维习惯去把握译写,从而取得更好的信息传递效果。

例5~7选自国内一个设计团队申请英国皇家艺术协会的景观园林设计遗产奖的申请报告(于2019年10月获奖)。这是一个讲好行业故事、传播中国传统文化和中国设计品牌形象的典型实例。

【分析1】

申报质量和读者接受程度有重要关系。

目标读者:英国皇家艺术协会的评审专家。

文本目标：推介设计团队将中国传统景观园林设计理念与现代技术和艺术创新相结合的实践成果，突出主题信息，以便从众多竞争者中胜出。

翻译策略：减少词汇和句式表达的复杂度，加强语篇的逻辑性和连贯性，注重表达的客观性，增强说服力。

【例5】

中国地域空间跨度广大，气候和地域文化的差异给整个国家的地理和人文环境风貌带来了极大的丰富性和差异性。在此背景之下的中国风景园林学科具有悠久的历史和传统，中国传统的风景园林大多数在地理的差异性之上都遵循了较为一致的文化传统的核心理念，以尊重自然作为其核心理念，重视处理好人与自然的和谐关系，并强调运用超越显性的物理空间形态的、艺术性极强的表达方式，来达成主题和场所精神的有效传达。因而，中国传统的风景园林呈现出与其他地域文化所不同的独特面貌，并且对未来人类生活的品质提升和社会的和谐发展具有特殊的文化价值，所以中国传统风景园林在当代的传承与发展是一个极有意义的重要课题。

Developed in a vast territory with a great diversity in climates, regional cultures and living environment, Chinese landscape architecture (CLA) boasts a time-honored history and tradition. Despite of geographic differences, traditional CLA follows the core concepts of traditional culture to achieve a harmony between man and nature, and aims at expressing the theme and the sense of place by means of an approach that goes beyond the dominant physical space or form and artistic expression. Therefore, traditional CLA, with its distinctive features, presents a cultural value that is inspiring for the improvement of human life and harmonious development of society. It is a significant issue to inherit and develop traditional CLA at present times.

郑捷先生及其团队立足于中国杭州——拥有西湖、良渚双遗产的城市，20余年来致力于对中国地域文化的研究、人文历史的挖掘，以及综合自然环境与人文要素的作品整体风貌的展示，完成了数十项建成的景观规划与设计项目，以其作品内在而独特的感染力，诠释了中国风景园林的审美传统和美学趣味，为中国传统风景园林学科的传承与发展做出了显著的贡献。

Zheng Jie and his team, based in Hangzhou—a city with heritages of West Lake and Liangzhu, have devoted themselves to the exploration of regional culture, history, and the display of comprehensive integration of natural environment with humanistic elements, completing dozens of landscape planning and design projects over the past 20 years. These works, with a strong appeal to emotion, have interpreted the aesthetic traditions and interests of CLA, which in turn contribute to the inheritance and development of traditional CLA. <u>Our efforts have achieved the significance in two aspects.</u>

【分析2】

第一段第一句的翻译省略了"给整个国家的地理和人文环境风貌带来了极大的丰富性和差异性",因为第二句提到"Despite of geographic differences";同样,"重视处理好人与自然的和谐关系"已经覆盖了"以尊重自然作为其核心理念",故删略重复性的表达。

第二段结尾增译"Our efforts have achieved the significance in two aspects.",为后面段落分两个方面论述其实践成果做铺垫(Uniqueness, Breakthrough, and Inheritance; Distinctive Features of Our Achievements)。

【例6】

(1) 我们立足于中国文化传统的传承与弘扬,完成了逾百项(包括未建成的)风景园林规划与设计实践,在服务于中国高速发展的社会经济、急迫的生态和文化建设的同时,也为世界风景园林学科更好地认识和吸收中国风景园林学科历史传统的有益价值,提供了积极而有说服力的实践案例。

Focusing on presenting and spreading traditional Chinese culture, we have completed over 100 landscape and garden planning and design projects (including those to be finished), committed ourselves to the service of rapid economic development, urgent ecological and cultural development in China. Our works can serve as convincing examples and inspiration for the development of LA elsewhere in the world.

一方面包括了大量<u>基于"天人合一"传统理念而采取的自然与人文完美融合策略的实践案例,以及在这些案例中运用的中国传统的在风景园林设计建设中通常且主要的特色手法</u>,为风景园林学科于实践中运用中国传统的理念和方法,提供了可称经典的示范。另一方面,大量以地域性、人文性为主题特征的风景园林规划与设计创作实践案例,在不同的社会层面带来了多方面广泛而积极的影响力,同时也为中国本土设计师的在地性创作提供了不同维度的创作方向的借鉴。

On the one hand, our works have adopted the approach typical of Chinese garden design, involving the idea of "integration of man and nature", which can serve as classical models for CLA practice. On the other hand, our works involve regional and humanistic themes, exerting great influence on various aspects of social life, and providing inspiration for Chinese designers.

（2）我们所运用的复合自然生态和人文生态的整体性实践理念，结合深度挖掘场地环境资源的价值和潜力的工作方法，符合主流的社会价值认识，对于长远而有效地解决中国社会高速发展所带来的错综复杂的社会矛盾和问题也必将发挥重要影响。我们的项目从建成的自然生态和环境景观效果到其后的日常运营，都产生了积极而明显的社会、生态和文化的综合效益，同时也显示出巨大而良好的可持续发展的价值和潜力。

We adopt a comprehensive approach involving natural and humanistic ecology, exploration of site environment and resources, in line with mainstream value, and keeping an eye on the long-term development, to address intricate contradictions and problems triggered by fast development. The operation and performance of our projects have proved to be positive and effective, and present a great value and potential for the sustainable development of society, ecology and culture.

（3）以杭州法云古村暨法云安缦酒店规划与设计、杭州西溪国家湿地公园规划与设计、杭州三台梦迹景区设计等一系列风景园林行业具有标杆性的作品为代表，我们引领了中国社会高速发展过程中传统村落的保护与利用、小型精品度假酒店的开发建设、国家湿地公园建设等与风景园林学科密切相关的项目类型的规划与设计创作的基本理念与实践方向，为风景园林行业在相关领域的创作实践提供了高水准而且可谓经典的示范，同时也获得了业内和业外乃至整个社会的高度认可与赞赏。

We are taking a lead in the protection and utilization of traditional villages, development of small boutique resort hotels and national wetland park, such as Amanfayun, Xixi National Wetland Park, and Santaimengji Scenic Spot in Hangzhou, to mention a few. Our works have won us fame in and outside the trade, serving as a benchmark for the industry.

【分析3】

在第（1）项陈述中，将"基于'天人合一'传统理念而采取的自然与人文完美融合策略的实践案例，以及在这些案例中运用的中国传统的在风景园林设计建设中通常且主要所采用的特色手法"概括为："our works have adopted the approach typical of Chinese garden design, involving the idea of 'integration of man and nature'"，减少理解难度。

在第（3）项陈述中，译文将"我们引领了"（We are taking a lead in...）作为主题句，然后以三个重点项目佐证（安缦酒店、西溪湿地公园、三台梦迹景区），意在说明我们这样的高水平设计比比皆是，然后得出结论：我们的设计为设计行业"提供了高水准而且可谓经典的示范"（serving as a benchmark for the industry）。结构清晰，主题信息突出，易于读者（评审专家）理解掌握。

与之相反，中文文本以三项重要设计起始，突出重点项目（代表作），然后得出结论："我们引领了……提供了高水准而且可谓经典的示范……"这样的论证思路，重点突出，结构清晰。但是，如果依照中文叙事思路翻译，就会产生这样的译文：

With such examples as the planning and designing of Amanfayun, Xixi National Wetland Park, and Santaimengji Spot in Hangzhou, which are the typical cases complying with the yardstick concerned, we've taken the lead in the basic concepts and direction in practice addressing planning and designing in a close tie with CLA. In response, our work is engaged in protection and deployment of old villages in the course of rapid growth of China, development and construction of small quality resort hotels, and national wetlands parks. Accordingly, our premium and classical examples are thus inspiring for innovative practice in the trade, winning high praises and appreciation within and outside the industry, even from the whole society.

这样的译文看似每一个细节都译出了，但是存在两个问题：一是内容凌乱，读者难以抓住重点信息；二是译文虽然突出了这三个经典项目，但是难免给人留下这样的感觉——这个团队也只有三个重点项目。

【例7】

（1）我们认为对于中国风景园林文化传统的认识理解和实践传承，必须先回到中国文化大传统的本源，<u>在本体论层面有所把握立足之后，才能真正地讨论在风景园林学科方面的传承与创新</u>。因而我们大量的本学科创作实践，首先是基于对中国文化传统本体论层面问题的探索与思考，进一步在本学科创作实践中加以认识论和方法论层面的展开。在我们大量画面感极强的唯美的工作成果背后，隐含了更宽泛的学科维度整合、更深刻的对于学科的本质思考。为此也需要我们在更多学科领域具有超越性的付出。

We believe the understanding and practice of the CLA is based on the comprehension of the essence of traditional Chinese culture. Most of our innovation and practice come from the exploration of traditional culture, consequently turning our observation and ideas into epistemology and methodology. Our aesthetic works with a strong visual appeal involve the integration of different discipline dimensions.

（2）我们在实践中综合自然生态和人文生态来系统地处理问题的理念，既符合风景园林学科的先进理念，也是对中国文化大传统本源的承接与把握。而以综合运用和组织场地环境中的各类显性或隐性的要素，结合艺术性的手法来实现对于项目主题和场所精神的特色表达，突出以超越物理空间形态来追求设计核心价值的意识和手法，更是体现了对中国风景园林学科独特小传统真正的认识理解和传承。

Our approach to natural and humanistic ecology not only conforms to the cutting-edge design concept of CLA, but also inherits traditional Chinese culture. We interpret and present the project theme and spirit of the site by means of artistic expression, as well as comprehensive utilization and organization of various visible and invisible elements of the site environment. This approach highlights the core design value that goes beyond the physical space and form, while presenting an understanding and inheritance of the CLA.

（3）我们的创作实践一贯以风景园林学科的基本理念和思路方法为主导，综合规划和建筑学科以及其他必要的专题研究，通过多学科工作流程的交叉复合、多维度专业知识的综合运用，有效而出色地完成了大量任务条件错综复杂、工作目标综合多样的项目任务要求，彰显了与其他团队完全不同的专业工作能力和创作潜力。

Our design practice, based on the basic concepts and ideas of LA, integrates planning, architecture and other disciplines, producing comprehensive solutions to address a diversity of complicated situations, manifesting our incomparable capability and potential to work within and cross teams or disciplines.

（4）受项目各种地域差异和建设成本控制等因素的影响，我们不得不面对大量的通过地方常规景观要素和素材来表达地域性、人文性的难题。我们总是以地域性常规的建造材料和传统的工艺，来加强项目所追求的独特魅力；同时，我们往往结合一定的现代建造技术手段和新型、更为高效的材料的使用，来提升项目的实际使用品质，进而实现设计整体目标的完美实现。

To cope with the challenge of regional differences and cost control, we make use of local landscape elements, construction materials and crafts to express the regional and humanistic features which highlight the uniqueness of our projects. Meanwhile, we adopt modern construction techniques and efficient use of new materials to improve the performance and overall quality of our projects.

［分析4］

为了便于读者快速理解掌握信息内容，译文对团队取得的成果做出概括性描述，略去枝节性和重复性陈述，突出重点信息；减少词汇和语句的复杂度，增强语篇的连贯性，提高译文的可读性和说服力。

例如，在第（1）项陈述中，删略没有实质性信息内容的画线部分的语句；将"我们大量的本学科创作实践，首先是基于对中国文化传统本体论层面问题的探索与思考，进一步在本学科创作实践中加以认识论和方法论层面的展开"概括为："Most of our innovation and practice come from the exploration of traditional culture, consequently turning our observation and ideas into epistemology and methodology."

此外还将"在我们大量画面感极强的唯美的工作成果背后，隐含了更宽泛的学科维度整合、更深刻的对于学科的本质思考。为此也需要我们在更多学科领域具有超越性的付出。"概括为："Our aesthetic works with a strong visual appeal involve the integration of different discipline dimensions."

参考文献

BARONE A, ANDERSON S. Total quality management [OL]. [2020-07-07]. https://www.investopedia.com/terms/t/total-quality-management-tqm.asp.

BENNETT J M. Intercultural competence [M]// CORTES C. (ed.). Multicultural America: A Multimedia Encyclopedia. Sage, 2013.

HONG T M, PIEKE F, STAM T. Chinese companies in the Netherlands [M]. Leiden: Leiden Asia Centre Press, 2017.

HOOKER J. Cultural differences in business communication [OL]. Tepper School of Business Carnegie Mellon University. [2008-12]. https://public.tepper.cmu.edu/jnh/businessCommunication.pdf.

MAHARJAN P. Intercultural Communication [OL]. [2018-01-09]. https://www.businesstopia.net/communication/intercultural-communicationUpdated.

McCluskey L. Professional culture shock [OL]. [2020-01-05]. http://www.healthyneurotics.com/professional-culture-shock/.

SEGAL T. The 4 stages of culture shock [OL]. [2019-09-01] https://medium.com/global-perspectives/the-4-stages-of-culture-shock-a79957726164.

TING-TOOMEYS. 跨文化间的交流 [M]. 上海：上海外语教育出版社，2007.

WÜRTZ E. Intercultural communication on web sites: a cross-cultural analysis of web sites from high-context cultures and low-context cultures [J]. Journal of Computer-Mediated Communication, 2005, 11 (1): 274 - 299.

贾文山. 如何打造均衡对等的中美谈判模式？：兼论如何跳出中美贸易谈判的陷阱 [J]. 腾胜全球文化，2019 (7).

卢小军. 中美网站企业概况的文本对比与外宣英译 [J]. 中国翻译，2012 (1).

马丁，那卡雅玛. 跨文化传播 [M]. 5版. 北京：清华大学出版社，2019.

潘一禾. 超越文化差异：跨文化交流的案例与探讨 [M]. 杭州：浙江大学出版社，2011.

史兴松. 中美企业网络商务话语跨文化研究 [C]. 首届全国商务话语学术研讨会，2021.

王立非. 上市企业年报话语质量对资本市场收益预测研究 [C]. 首届全国商务话语学术研讨会, 2021.

周小微, 陈永丽. 跨文化间的交流 [M]. 北京：对外经济贸易大学出版社, 2008.

庄恩平. 跨文化商务沟通案例教程 [M]. 上海：上海外语教育出版社, 2004.